RULES

Rules for **U**sing **L**inguistic **E**lements of **S**peech

A Resource and Interactive Workbook

Student Workbook

Marjorie Feinstein-Whittaker, M.S.
Lynda Katz Wilner, M.S.

COVER DESIGN: Sarah Bishins

RULES
Rules for Using Linguistic Elements of Speech
A Resource and Interactive Workbook

ISBN 0-9717038-2-5

Published by
Successfully Speaking
Owings Mills, MD 21117
410-356-5666   FAX 410-356-5666

Suggestions on How to Use the Audio CDs

There is an add-on option for five audio CDs corresponding to the 23 RULES described in this workbook.

As you look in each chapter, you will see a headphone icon to the left of the recorded information. The CD number and track will also be indicated.

The target words and sentences that appear on the CD are indicated by *italics* in your workbook.

The overview of the RULE is a **listen only** activity. Following a summary explanation, you will hear a series of stimulus words and sentences. You will hear one item at a time, followed by a brief pause. Repeat the word or sentence as clearly as you can during these pauses. For the sentences, it is recommended that you follow along with your workbook.

Try to match the trainer's production as closely as you can. Say the key word or sentence using the same clear, slow speech emphasizing the pronunciation and/or intonation rule.

Consistent, daily practice using the audio CDs and your workbook exercises will facilitate your transition to a more natural sounding, North American English style of speech.

Work hard and have fun!

CD #1 pages 3-45

CD #2 pages 47-88

CD #3 pages 89-126

CD#4 pages 127-161

CD#5 pages 161-200

RULES

Rules for Using Linguistic Elements of Speech

A Resource and Interactive Workbook

Student Workbook

Table of Contents

Introducing Yourself (Pre- and Post-Speech Samples)

Fill in the blanks on this form and make it grammatically correct. Then, using a recording device, record yourself reading the introduction aloud. Repeat this introductory passage after completing your training and compare the pre- and post-recordings.

Good morning/afternoon/evening. My name is _____. I was born in

_____ on _____. I went to _____

(city/state/province/country)   (birth date)   (college/university)

in _____ and earned a _____ in the field of _____.

(city/state/country)   (degree abbreviation)

I graduated in _____. I currently work as _____ at

(date)   (job title)

_____ in _____, _____.

(company)   (city)   (state)

My first language is _____ and I've been speaking English for _____

years. My biggest communication challenge is

_____

_____.

I will consider this training program a success if, at the end, I will be able

to_____. I know that with a positive attitude

I will make a lot of progress.

My home address is _____ in _____, _____
                        (street)   (city)   (state)

and my telephone number is _____. My e-mail address is

_____.

Thank you very much.

The American Sound System

American English is composed of consonants and vowels. The International Phonetic Alphabet (IPA) is a set of universal symbols that represent each and every sound in the speech of any language. The consonant (Figure 1) and vowel (Figure 2) sound systems are displayed on the accompanying charts. In order to make the words in this program easier to read, attempts have been made to avoid the use of the IPA symbols unless necessary. However, knowledge of these symbols makes it easy to transcribe and understand different pronunciations of the same word and will be used when needed.

Consonant Sound System

International Phonetic Alphabet

CD
1:2

Figure 1

Place of Production

Manner of Production		Labial	Labio-Dental	Dental	Alveolar	Palatal	Velar	Glottal
	Stop-Plosive	p b̲			t d̲		k g̲	
	Fricative		f v̲	θ ð̲	s z̲	ʃ ʒ		h
	Affricate					tʃ d̲ʒ		
	Glides	w̲				r̲ j		
	Lateral				l̲			
	Nasal	m̲			n̲		ŋ	

The underlined sounds in this chart are produced with voice. All others are voiceless.

Key:

ʃ	= *shoe*	tʃ	= *church*	dʒ = *judge*	j	= *yellow*
ʒ	= *measure*	θ	= *think*	ŋ = *sing*	ð	= *father*

Consonants are categorized according to their:
- **place of production**
- **manner of production**
- **voicing**

The **place of production** focuses on the articulators that are used to make the sound. Sounds may be produced at the lips (**labial**), such as /p/, /b/, /w/, and /m/. They can be produced with the teeth resting on the lips and are called **labio-dental** sounds and include /f/ and /v/. **Dental** sounds are produced with the tongue resting between the teeth and include /θ/ as in "<u>th</u>ink" and /ð/ as in "fa<u>th</u>er." **Alveolar** sounds are produced by having the tongue tip rest behind the upper teeth on the alveolar ridge. These sounds are /t/, /d/, /s/, /z/, /l/, and /n/. The **palatal** sounds are produced with the lateral margins of the tongue up against the hard palate and include /ʃ/ as in "shoe," /ʒ/ as in "mea<u>s</u>ure," /tʃ/ as in "chur<u>ch</u>," /dʒ/ as in "ju<u>dg</u>e," /r/ as in "<u>r</u>ed," and /j/ as in "<u>y</u>ellow." The **velar** sounds are produced with the back of the tongue up against the soft palate or velum. These sounds are /k/, /g/, and /ŋ/, as in "si<u>ng</u>." Finally, the **glottal** sound is produced by allowing air to pass through the glottis or vocal cords and the only sound produced in this manner is /h/.

Consonants can also be described by the **manner** in which they are produced. **Stop-plosives** stop the air stream momentarily and then release it. Those sounds are: /p/, /b/, /t/, /d/, /k/, and /g/. **Fricatives** are produced by forcing the air stream through a narrow passage and creating friction in the vocal tract and include /f/, /v/, /θ/, /ð/, /s/, /z/, /ʃ/, /ʒ/, and /h/. **Affricates** are a combination between stop-plosives and fricatives and include /tʃ/ and /dʒ/. **Nasal** sounds, /m/, /n/, and /ŋ/ are produced as the air stream is directed through the nasal passage. **Glides** move towards the vowel sound that follows and include /w/, /r/, and /j/. The **lateral** sound /l/ is produced as the air stream is directed over both sides of the tongue.

Many of the sounds are arranged as pairs. Within a pair, one sound is produced without any vocal cord vibration (**voiceless**), and the other has vocal cord vibration (**voiced**). The underlined sounds are voiced.

Vowel Sound System

Figure 2

Place of Production

	Front	Central	Back
High	[i] (beat)		[u] (boot)
	[ɪ] (bit)	[ɝ] (bird) [ɚ] (memb<u>er</u>)	[ʊ] (book)
Middle	[e] (bait)	[ʌ] (but)	[o] (boat)
		[ə] (<u>a</u>bove)	
	[ɛ] (bet)		[ɔ] (bought)
Low	[æ] (bat)		[ɑ] (box)

lips retracted   **lips rounded**

Although there are only five letters for vowels in the English language, there are many more vowel <u>sounds</u>. For this reason, phonetic symbols are used to describe each of the sounds. Production of vowels involves the tongue, lip, and jaw positioning. The tip of the tongue rests against the back of the lower teeth for <u>all</u> vowel sounds. The tongue height can be high, middle, or low and the tongue position can be towards the front, in the central position of the mouth, or pulled back in the mouth. The lips are somewhat retracted for the front vowels and rounded for the back vowels. Diphthongs can be produced by combining two vowels together, e.g., [aɪ] as in "bye," [aʊ] as in "how," and [ɔɪ] as in "boy." Figure 2 shows sample words for each of the phonetic symbols.

Stress and Intonation Rules

1. Compound Noun Stress Patterns

**CD
1:3**

A compound noun is comprised of two distinct words that are joined together to create a word with a new meaning. They can be written as one new word, e.g., checkbook, airport; they may be two separate words, e.g., bank account, parking lot; or they may be hyphenated, e.g., drive-thru, take-out. To determine which form is accurate, consult a dictionary. The list of compound words is exhaustive and new words arise as our technology changes.

*The first <u>word</u> of a compound noun should be stressed with a <u>higher</u> pitch, <u>louder</u> volume and <u>longer</u> vowel. If the first word has two or more syllables, remember to maintain the correct syllable stress for that word, e.g., **<u>Emer</u>gency** Room, **<u>Insur</u>ance** card. There may be regional differences for stressed syllables.*

Exercise 1: Read the following compound words aloud. Be sure to stress the first word in the pair, saying it with *higher* pitch, *louder* volume and a *longer* vowel. Then, try to make up your own sentences using the compound words that you usually use. Add some of your own terms to the lists under **Personal Words**.

**CD
1:4**

Computer-related terms

download	upgrade	shortcut	keyboard
screensaver	password	username	login
logout	backspace	e-mail	software
hardware	desktop	laptop	headset
Microsoft®	QuickBooks®	Spyware®	Paintshop®
PowerPoint®	chat room	word count	control key
endpoint	soundcard	thumb drive	megabytes
terabytes	webpage	mainframe	motherboard
webcam	backup	address book	firewall
hyperlink	clipboard	underscore	backslash
forward slash	memory stick	floppy disc	zip drive
clip art	hard drive	virus scan	web address
spell check	hotmail	inbox	outbox
pop-up	mailbox	junk mail	network

benchmark	barcode	dial-up	high speed
Personal Words			

Travel and Transportation Terms

CD 1:4

travel agent	airline	airplane	sightseeing
train station	suitcase	airport	tourist trap
check-in	boarding pass	layover	non-stop
heliport	car keys	tollbooth	toll collector
fast lane	bus station	ticket agent	one-way
round trip	skycap	baggage claim	parking garage
underground	subway	overpass	highway
causeway	turnpike	timeshare	beltway
throughway	underpass	EZpass^{SM}	parking pass
windshield wipers	gas tank	oil filter	garage door
tune-up	oil change	tire pressure	fluid levels
blow out	seatbelt	airbag	car insurance
meal plan	passport	rush hour	money order
traveler's checks	credit card	debit card	flight insurance
passing lane	express lane		
Personal Words			

Work-related Terms

CD 1:4

conference room	training room	parking lot	discussion group
press conference	overtime	full-time	part-time
teamwork	team leader	workday	workload
workplace	outcome	dinner meeting	lunchtime
start-up	chairman	reception area	break room
boardroom	network	carpool	office supplies

mailroom	paycheck	sick leave	sick days
workshop	appointment book	briefcase	Palm Pilot™
textbook	timeline	executive board	break-out rooms
circuit breaker	distribution center	fire door	board members
fax machine	copy machine	fire extinguisher	speakerphone
work station	voice over	Wall Street	status report
Stock Exchange	stockbroker	salesman	businessman
downsize	fiscal year	line graph	bar graph
pie chart	small talk	time clock	timesheet
showroom	wholesale	high-tech	decision making
business trip	weekday	weekend	power cord
Personal Words			

Home-related Terms

real estate	property tax	homeowner's	title search
bedroom	family room	screen door	living room
bathroom	sitting room	dressing room	fireplace
penthouse	housekeeper	grounds keeper	landscaper
clothesline	doghouse	playroom	water heater
skylight	driveway	carport	air conditioning
sidewalk	landlord	upstairs	downstairs
doorknob	lawn mower	snow blower	lawn care
window treatment	china closet	coffee maker	teacup
Personal words			

Communication Terms

newspaper	newscast	voiceover	web cast
anchorman	weatherman	cell phone	answering machine

voicemail	Blackberry ™	headline	speaker phone
cover story	dateline	deadline	freelance
press release	byline	sidebar	wire service
movie reviews	proofread	copy editor	tape recorder

Personal words

Financial Terms

checkbook	cash flow	passbook	deposit slip
bank statement	savings account	money market	stock market
balance sheet	checking account	bank teller	loan officer
branch office	maintenance fee	debit card	credit card
service charge	income tax	tax return	tax refund
finance charge	late fee	transfer fee	bank account

Personal Words

Hygiene Terms

haircut	hairdresser	shaving cream	make-up
lipstick	toothpaste	toothbrush	mouthwash
restroom	bathroom	Men's room	Ladies' room
razor blades	cream rinse	sunscreen	sun block
blow-dry	touch-up	washcloth	hairbrush
cotton ball	Q-tip®	hairspray	hair dryer
nail clippers	nail file	emery board	nail polish

Personal Words

Sports Terms

golf course	tennis courts	golf cart	football
basketball	locker room	pro shop	ballgame
baseball	racquetball	workout	kick off
field goal	halfback	shoot out	quarterback
end zone	cheerleader	penalty kick	rain delay
headline	wrap-up	touchdown	ski resort
downhill	snowboard	snowshoes	ice skates
ski boots	chairlift	car racing	body building
field hockey	horseback riding	mountain climbing	scuba diving
weight lifting	weight training	skateboard	bike path
diving board	goalkeeper	ticket sales	running shoes

Personal Words

Medical Terms

blood pressure	vital signs	Emergency Room	waiting room
chest pain	blood test	headache	stomachache
toothache	check-up	pacemaker	eyeglasses
wheelchair	blood work	bed rest	health insurance
drug abuse	substance abuse	immune system	organ transplant
stem cells	painkillers	office hours	insurance card
office visit	co-pay	health form	heat stroke
wound care	breast cancer	well visit	lab fees
side effects	sick visit	ace bandage	Band-Aid®

Personal Words

Social/Recreation Terms

book club	playground	birthday	greeting card
birthday cake	gift certificate	gift card	early bird
happy hour	baby shower	bridal party	rehearsal dinner
guest list	bachelor party	thank-you notes	response card
takeout	drive-thru	drive-in	carryout
delivery man	birthday party	slumber party	sleepover
nightmare	daydream	bike helmet	cocktail party
dinner party	lifestyle	block party	party favor

Personal Words

Weather Terms

summertime	wintertime	springtime	raincoat
snowstorm	thunderstorm	downpour	sunlight
moonlight	sunglasses	daytime	nighttime
raindrops	suntan	sunburn	frostbite
sandstorm	hailstorm	snowflakes	snowman
snowfall	hurricane season	snowball	mudslide

Personal Words

People

grandmother	grandfather	mother-in-law	sister-in-law
stepson	stepdaughter	someone	somebody
anybody	no one	anyone	everyone
step-father	step-mother	half-brother	half-sister
godmother	godfather	godparents	babysitter

Personal Words

School Terms

homework	school bus	playground	report card
bathroom	restroom	lunchroom	book report
term paper	notebook	loose leaf	pencil sharpener
ballpoint	gum eraser	backpack	book bag
decimal point	book review	computer games	progress report
vacation week	blackboard	flagpole	textbook
preschool	middle school	high school	elementary school
carpool	classroom	classmate	outline
paperback	playmate	placement exam	guidance counselor
honor roll	honor society	social studies	varsity sports

Personal Words

Around the Town Terms

parking meter	parking ticket	fire station	police station
meter maid	art gallery	shoe store	post office
jewelry store	drugstore	book store	movie theater
toy store	liquor store	parking garage	sporting goods store
household	housework	grocery store	hardware store
carpool	sandpaper	delivery man	highchair
mailman	street sign	lamppost	clock tower
senior center	town hall*	dry cleaners*	art center
shopping center	garden center	coffee shop	fitness center
body shop	taxi stand	pet store	car wash
travel agent	gas station	craft shop	flower shop
medical center	office park	doctor's office	shopping mall
strip mall	bus stop	subway stop	bus station
animal hospital	recording studio	dance studio	hair salon
picnic tables	recreation center	skating rink	shoe repair

Some words may be pronounced as a compound noun or an adjective + noun

.Personal Words

Food Terms

breakfast	cottage cheese	ice cream	junk food
leftovers	pancakes	popcorn	potato chips
shellfish	main course	milkshake	whipped cream*
*skim milk**	iced tea*	lemonade	cheesecake
*french fries**	hamburger	cheeseburger	hotdog
cream cheese	Swiss cheese	American cheese	sour cream

Some words may be pronounced as a compound noun or an adjective + noun.

Personal Words

Clothing Terms

raincoat	sunglasses	ski jacket	shoelaces
bathing suit	tee-shirt	overcoat	bathrobe
backpack	wedding gown	sun hat	sundress
running shoes	sweat suit	sweatshirt	long johns
nightgown	windbreaker	ski boots	ski pants

Personal Words

Exercise 2: Practice reading the following sentences and focus on the stress pattern for the compound words. First, underline the compound words in each sentence. Then, read them aloud using correct compound noun stress patterns. **NOTE:** Phrasal verbs are noted with an asterisk *. Remember to use the correct stress pattern (stress the second word). Please see Unit 2 (Compound Nouns vs. Phrasal Verbs) for more information.

1. *Go to the website and enter your user id and password.*
2. *Hand the bank teller your deposit slip and paycheck.*
3. *Do you have a desktop or a laptop in your office?*
4. *I'll use my gift certificate for the early bird special at the restaurant.*
5. *Should we eat in the boardroom or the conference room?*
6. Did you run your virus scan and install a firewall to protect your hard drive?
7. Do you want to pay with a debit card or credit card?

8. I lost my car keys in the parking lot before the workshop.

9. Our discussion group will meet to review the PowerPoint.

10. I need to upgrade my QuickBooks® program before I print out * the balance sheet.

11. Back up* your data on a memory stick or a floppy disc before you log out.*

12. Let's go during "Happy Hour" to celebrate your birthday.

13. How many megabytes or gigabytes can your mainframe handle?

14. Do I type in* a backslash or a forward slash for your web address?

15. Your supervisor will distribute new clipboards, notebooks, and headsets to all new team members.

16. Click your keyboard to activate your screensaver.

17. The loan officer at this branch office is retiring.

18. Call the travel agent to book a timeshare for the summertime.

19. Should we meet at the golf course or the tennis courts?

20. Let's buy a round trip instead of a one-way.

21. Order take-out for the dinner meeting.

22. In the bathroom, you'll find extra shaving cream, toothpaste, a toothbrush, soap, and towels.

23. Take an aspirin if you have a headache, toothache, or stomachache.

24. Has anybody seen my appointment book or my briefcase?

25. I have a parking pass for the underground parking lot.

26. The halfback scored a touchdown at the football game.

27. There was a rain delay due to the thunderstorm.

28. After double overtime, they had a shoot out.

29. Do you play racquetball or basketball?

30. He told the bank teller that he lost his passbook for his savings account.

NOTE: Some of these word pairs may be spoken with alternate word stress patterns. Be sure to stress at least one of the words; for example, one-**way** vs. **one**-way.

2. Compound Nouns vs. Phrasal Verbs

CD 1:6

Compound nouns are two distinct words that are joined together to create a word with a new meaning, and the stress is usually on the **first** part of the word. We often hyphenate compound nouns, e.g., make-up, get-away.

Phrasal verbs are two to three words combined to make up a phrase with a new and different meaning. They can be semantically and grammatically complex and can be classified as transitive or intransitive. Transitive phrasal verbs take an object (Please walk **down** the steps). Intransitive phrasal verbs <u>cannot</u> take a direct object (I'd like to sit **down**). Phrasal verbs may also be separable (give it **away**) or inseparable (give **away**). Phrasal verbs can have literal or figurative interpretations. The stress pattern is on the **second** part of the verb. Sometimes the phrasal verb is broken up by a word between, e.g., **back** it **up**.

Example:

*Compound Noun: After a long month of work, we found a wonderful **get**-away.*

*Phrasal Verb: Let's get **away** for the weekend and forget about our worries.*

*Get it **away** from the window.*

NOTE: The notations above illustrate the correct stress patterns for the examples. Remember to maintain the correct sentence level stress pattern. If you over exaggerate the phrasal verb, the rhythm of the sentence will be disrupted.

In this exercise, we will be discussing the two-part inseparable phrasal verb. For more information, please consult a grammar book.

Exercise 1: Underline the word that should receive the stress in the following sentences. Then, practice saying each sentence aloud. Focus on the correct stress pattern and remember to link the words together.

1. ***Trade in***
    A. *What do you think you can get as a trade in for your old car?*
    B. *I need to trade in my hand mixer for an electric one.*

CD 1:7

2. *Print out*
   A. Please give me a print out of the new polices and procedures.
   B. Can you please print out the e-mail for me?

3. *Log in*
   A. What is the password to log in?
   B. Something is wrong with my computer; I can't log in anymore.
   C. Do you have a log in password?

4. *Make up*
   A. Is there a make up available if the weather conditions are poor?
   B. I purchased new make up for the spring season.
   C. Let's kiss and make up.
   D. Just make up an answer if you aren't sure!

5. *Check in*
   A. The hotel said check in time was at 11 a.m.
   B. Is it okay if I check in with you when my plane arrives?

6. Check out
   A. I'll meet you at the check out line.
   B. Did you check out the new fall clothing line by Calvin Klein?

7. Back up
   A. Please back up your programs at the end of every workday.
   B. As a back up, I like to keep bottled water in the garage.

8. Take out
   A. Let's order Chinese take out for dinner tonight.
   B. Please take out the garbage on your way to work.

9. Break out
   A. Why do I always break out before an important meeting?
   B. The horse will break out of the stable during the storm.
   C. Let's have the break out session before lunch.

10. Fill in
   A. The test is multiple choice, fill in and essay.
   B. She's the fill in for the gym teacher this week.
   C. She went to the manicurist for a fill in.
   D. Please fill in the form as completely as possible.

11. Hold up
   A. What seems to be the hold up in getting the deliveries on time?
   B. Did you hear there was a hold up at the bank?
   C. Hold up the gift so we can all see it.

12. Hang up
    A. Hang up the phone in the kitchen, please.
    B. Why is there always a hang up when you call customer service?

13. Try out
    A. I will try out for the team, but the competition is fierce.
    B. He was very nervous for the team try outs.
    C. Try out this new fountain pen.

14. Phase out
    A. They are trying to phase out that particular product line.
    B. We are in the final stages of the phase out.

15. Buy out
    A. Did you buy out the entire store?
    B. Is it a buyout or a merger they're talking about?

16. Pick up
    A. Can you please pick up the package at the post office?
    B. Let's pick up this conversation where we left off yesterday.
    C. That was quite an unusual pick up line.

17. Mix up
    A. Mix up the batter so it won't be lumpy.
    B. There was a terrible mix up in the accounting office.

18. Put down
    A. I can't believe what a put down that was!
    B. Put down those heavy packages before you hurt yourself.

19. Give away
    A. Give away your old clothes to charity.
    B. I got all these prizes as a give away at the store opening.

20. Turn off
    A. Turn off the iron when you are finished ironing.
    B. That combination of food is such a turn off.

3. Adjective + Noun Stress Patterns

CD
1:8

*In a sentence with an adjective + noun, the **noun** is stressed, e.g., "red **car**."*

Sometimes the same two words can make up a compound noun, or have a completely different meaning as an adjective + noun combination.

*With a compound noun, the stress is on the **first** word, e.g., greenhouse.*
*With an adjective + noun, the **noun** is stressed, e.g., green **house**.*

1. Compound word (stress on the first word)

> *"He grows plants in a **green**house."*

> *"Let's take a tour of the **White** House."*

2. Adjective + noun (stress on the noun)

> *"He lives in a green **house**."*

> *"I live in a white **house** with yellow shutters."*

<u>One</u> *of the words should be stressed; you should not stress both nor have both unstressed.*

CD
1:9

Exercise 1: Say the following word pairs and stress the appropriate word. Think about the different meanings of each pair and create a sentence to highlight the intended meaning.

NOTE: Remember, compound nouns can be written as one word, two separate words, or with a hyphen. Consult a dictionary if you are unsure. Remember, there may be regional differences for stress patterns and pronunciation.

Compound Noun	Adjective + Noun
*green*house	green *house*
*black*board	black *board*
*white*board	white *board*
short-term	short *term*
long-term	long *term*
yellow jacket	yellow **jacket**
orange juice	orange **juice**
blue collar	blue **collar**
white collar	white **collar**
Green Beret	green **beret**
firewall	fire **wall**
yellowtail	yellow **tail**
black and **blue** mark	black and blue **marks**
West Wing	west **wing**
Rose Garden	rose **garden**
Oval Office	oval **office**
Southside	south **side**
Eastside	east **side**
wise guy	wise **guy**
fat cat	fat **cat**
short order	short **order**
overtime	over **time**
hard hat	hard **hat**

Compound Noun	Adjective + Noun
Bigboy™	big **boy**
Lazyboy™	lazy **boy**
lowdown	low **down**
Red Line	red **line**
tan line	tan **line**
pink slip	pink **slip**
bluebook	blue **book**
Pink Eye	pink **eye**

Exercise 2: Complete each sentence using the appropriate compound noun or adjective plus noun response.

CD
1:10

---

1.   a. **pink** slip   b. pink **slip**

Mary bought a beautiful _____ to wear under her silk gown.

I hope I don't get a _____ during the upcoming round of layoffs.

---

2.   a. **Red** Line   b. red **line**

You can take the _____ to Harvard Square.

Please draw a _____ down the left hand side of the paper.

---

3.   a. **white**board   b. white **board**

Elana drew the organizational chart on the _____ in the conference room.

Steven took the_____ into the garage to make a poster.

---

4.   a. **tan** line   b. tan **line**

The construction crew painted a _____ around the perimeter of the building.

Grace came home from vacation with a funny _____ on her arms.

---

5.   a. **Rose** *Garden*   b. *rose* **garden**

The President met with the foreign leaders in the _____.

This spring I am going to plant a beautiful _____.

---

6.   a. **yellow**tail   b. yellow **tail**

The cute puppy had brown eyes and a _____.

Let's go out for sushi and order _____ and tuna sashimi.

---

7.   a. **yellow** jacket   b. yellow **jacket**

Janya wore white jeans and a _____ to the picnic.

I was stung by a _____ on my hand this afternoon.

---

8.   a. **fat** cat   b. fat **cat**

If you keep feeding Helen all of those liver treats, she'll become a _____.

Ken's a _____ at his company.

---

9.   a. **hard** hat   b. hard **hat**

Please keep out of the _____ area!

The batter needs to wear a _____ so he doesn't get hit in the head with a bad pitch.

---

10.   a. **over**time   b. over **time**

_____, I think they will adjust to living on the East Coast.

Do you get _____ if you work on the weekends?

---

11.   a. **low**down   b. low **down**

Let's get the _____ on the party plans.

You have to crawl _____ to see the baby animal in it's nest.

---

12.   a. **white** collar   b. white **collar**

Jin has a _____ job as an executive officer.

My blouse has white cuffs and a _____.

---

13.   a. **Green** Beret   b. green **beret**

Do you like how this _____ looks with my coat?

Mimi's uncle was a patriot and a _____ for twenty years.

---

14.   a. **wise** guy   b. wise **guy**

Tony Soprano plays a _____ in the hit HBO series.

Mike's math and science teacher is an extremely _____ .

---

15.   a. **blue** collar   b. blue **collar**

Maria's shirt was striped with a _____ .

Sam didn't like to be called a _____ worker.

Exercise 3: The words in bold are pronounced using either the compound noun or adjective + noun stress pattern. Underline the word in each group that should receive the primary stress. There may be some examples where either pattern is acceptable. Then, say the sentences aloud and focus on the stress pattern.

A: Have you heard the **weather report** for today?
B: Yes, it is supposed to be cloudy with a chance of **thunderstorms**.
A: Oh, I was hoping it would be a **sunny day**, for a change!

A: May I offer you some coffee and a **homemade oatmeal cookie**?
B: A **coffee break** sounds lovely, thank you!
A: Do you drink **regular** or **decaffeinated coffee**?

A: School starts next week! What **school supplies** do you still need to buy?
B: I have **everything** except a **pocket dictionary** and **manila folders**.
A: Fine. Are you sure that you have enough **No. 2 pencils** and **lined paper**?

A: What are your plans on this **unseasonably warm day**?
B: I have to mow the **front lawn** and fix the **tire swing**.
A: And then what?
B: I am going to the **swimming pool** at 3:00 p.m. for the adult **free swim**.

A: Would you like to come running with me on this **crisp** and **cool day**?
B: Okay. What route are you planning to take?
A: I thought I would do 5 miles on the **jogging path** at the **high school track**.

A: Whom are you inviting to the **graduation party**?
B: Oh, our **next-door neighbors**, **old friends** and family from out of town.
A: That sounds great! Please give Tom our **best wishes**!

A: Please do your **household chores** before you go to work!

B: What would you like me to do?

A: Change the sheets and **pillowcases**, put on the **bedspread**, and put out **clean towels** in the **bathroom**.

A: Are you going to the **Little League game** this **afternoon**?

B: Yes, I'll be sitting in the **bleacher seats**.

A: I'll head over after our church's **picnic lunch** in the park.

A: We have a meeting with our **financial planner** next week.

B: What's on the agenda?

A: We have to talk about liquidating some assets, updating our **insurance policies** and an IRA **rollover**.

A: What would you like for **breakfast**?

B: I think I'll have some **orange juice**, **scrambled eggs** and **fresh fruit**.

A: Let me clean the **counter top** and load the **dishwasher** so I have room to prepare **everything**!

A: I have a meeting with a **high-end client** this morning.

B: Why do you look so **uptight**?

A: We are discussing a **large investment** and I hope that it goes well.

A: We are in the process of planning our **winter vacation**.

B: What exotic locations or **get-aways** are you considering?

C: Someplace with **gentle breezes** and **mild weather**!

A: Please park your car in the **driveway**.

B: Okay, but I don't want to block the bicycles and **motorcycle**.

A: Yes, and don't run over the **garbage cans** or the **recycling bins**!

A: Are Jayden and Sasha ready for their **ballet recital**?

B: I still have to put on their **make-up** and fix their hair with **bobby pins**.

A: Their **ballet slippers** and **toe shoes** are in their **backpacks**!

A: Did your brother put the **log cabin** on the market?

B: No, but he is thinking about having an **open house** this **weekend**.

A: With **ski season** around the corner, it is a good time to see what the market will bear.

A: Are you ready to go on your **business trip**?

B: My **suitcase** is packed and I have the **airline tickets** and **passports** in my **briefcase**.

A: I'll meet you on the **front porch** in 5 minutes and drive you to the **airport**.

4. Proper Nouns

CD
1:11

*Proper nouns are geographical locations such as continents, countries, states, cities, islands, bodies of water, parks, roadways, mountains, tourist attractions, museums, hospitals, airlines or cruise lines, sports teams, publications, and people's names and titles. In two word proper nouns, each name is spelled with a capital letter and the stress is on the second word; for example, Los **Angeles** is one of the largest cities in Southern **California**.*

*An exception to this rule is the stress pattern for streets, which stresses the first word; for example, **Smith** Street vs. Park **Avenue**.*

Exercise 1: Read the words aloud, stressing the correct word. Make up your own sentences and add any words to your **personal word lists**.

Continents

North America	South America

CD
1:12

Countries

Great Britain	Costa Rica	New Zealand
Dominican Republic	Puerto Rico	El Salvador
North Korea	Saudi Arabia	South Korea
Vatican City	Ivory Coast	Sierra Leone
South Africa	Upper Volta	New Guinea

States

New Jersey	New York	New Mexico
New Hampshire	Rhode Island	North Carolina
North Dakota	South Carolina	South Dakota
West Virginia		

Geographic Locations

Mid-Atlantic	New England	Cape Cod

Mid-West	Southwest	Far East
Mid-East	Western Hemisphere	North Pole
Cape Ann	Desert Valley	Upper East Side
Back Bay	Metro West	Central Europe
Northern Ireland	Lower Saxony	New South Wales
West Flanders	Middle East	Southern California
South Pole	Squaw Valley	Southeast Asia

Cities

Los Angeles	San Francisco	New Brunswick
New Orleans	Fort Worth	New Delhi
Colorado Springs	Las Vegas	Chapel Hill
St. Paul	Fort Knox	Grand Rapids
Cape May	Cape Canaveral	Daytona Beach
Fort Lauderdale	Great Falls	Palm Beach
Park City	Silver Spring	San Diego
Owings Mills	Grosse Point	Rio de Janeiro
New Rochelle	Key Biscayne	Des Moines
New York City	San Jose	San Antonio
Miami Beach	Key West	New Haven
Monte Carlo	San Juan	The Hague
New Bedford	New Salem	Cape Town
Tampa Bay	East Lansing	Palo Alto

Islands

Long Island	Grand Cayman Islands	Block Island
Virgin Islands	Coney Island	Fire Island
Staten Island	Ellis Island	Sanibel Island
Captiva Island	Roosevelt Island	Hawaiian Islands

Bodies of Water

Atlantic Ocean	Pacific Ocean	Indian Ocean

Baltic Sea	Mediterranean Sea	Long Island Sound
Lake Michigan	Red Sea	Lake Champlain
Arctic Ocean	Lake Placid	Lake Huron
Chesapeake Bay	Mississippi River	Charles River
Pearl Harbor	San Francisco Bay	Lake Superior
Hudson River	Colorado River	Lake Como
Lake Tahoe	Snake River	Lake Ontario
St. Lawrence Seaway	Suez Canal	Panama Canal
English Channel	Irish Sea	Swan Lake
Dead Sea	Black Sea	Amazon River
Yellow River	Nile River	Yangtze River

Parks / Mountains / Tourist Attractions / Museums

Central Park	United Nations	Longwood Gardens
Mt. Rushmore	Statue of Liberty	Yosemite National Park
Smithsonian Institution	National Gallery	Yellowstone National Park
Tower of London	Westminster Abbey	Niagara Falls
Rocky Mountains	Appalachian Mountains	Mount Hood
Bear Mountain	Green Mountains	The Alps
Mt. McKinley	Mt. Everest	Mt. St. Helens
Eiffel Tower	Guggenheim Museum	Grand Canyon
Holocaust Museum	Museum of History	Metropolitan Opera
Lincoln Memorial	Museum of Fine Arts	Washington Monument
Tate Gallery	Museum of Science	Baseball Hall of Fame
Football Hall of Fame	Vatican Museum	National Aquarium
Buckingham Palace	Taj Mahal	Mount Fuji
Great Wall of China	Big Ben	Children's Museum
Acadia National Park	Vatican City	San Diego Zoo
White Mountains	Mount Washington	Quincy Market
Universal Studios	Fells Point	Inner Harbor

Roadways (except Street)

Golden Gate Bridge	Midtown Tunnel	Chesapeake Bay Bridge
Fifth Avenue	Constitution Avenue	Martin Luther King Blvd.
Rodeo Drive	Route One	George Washington Bridge
New Jersey Turnpike	Penny Lane	Esgarth Way
Long Island Expressway	Belt Parkway	New York Thruway
Avenue of the Americas	Park Avenue	The Royal Mile
Apian Way	Lexington Avenue	Madison Avenue

Hospitals

Johns Hopkins	Mass General	Mayo Clinic
Thomas Jefferson	Good Samaritan	Sloan Kettering
Cedar Sinai	St. Vincent's	Chicago Rehabilitation
Dana Farber	Columbia Presbyterian	St. Jude's Hospital

Cruise Lines / Airlines

Royal Caribbean	Holland America	Air France
American Airlines	Jet Blue	Aer Lingus
Delta Airlines	British Airways	Virgin Airways
Air India	El Al	Southwest Airways

Sports Teams / Events

World Cup	World Series	Indianapolis 500
March Madness	US Open	San Antonio Spurs
Boston Celtics	Baltimore Blast	Detroit Pistons
Boston Red Sox	Seattle Seahawks	Philadelphia Flyers
New York Yankees	Philadelphia Eagles	Baltimore Orioles
Green Bay Packers	Pittsburgh Steelers	Dallas Cowboys
Miami Dolphins	Montreal Maple Leafs	Boston Bruins
Chicago Blackhawks	New York Rangers	Kentucky Derby
Belmont Stakes	Montreal Canadians	Tour de France

©2006, RULES

Indianapolis 500	Los Angeles Lakers	Houston Rockets
Chicago White Sox	New York Jets	New England Patriots
Manchester United	Real Madrid	Grand Prix

People

George Washington	Abraham Lincoln	Thomas Jefferson
Albert Einstein	Dr. Spock	Mrs. Robinson
Mr. President	Queen Elizabeth	Prince William
Princess Diana	King Tut	Sir Lawrence Olivier
Governor Winthrop	Senator Kennedy	Prime Minister Thatcher
Paul Newman	Katherine Hepburn	Anthony Hopkins
Sir Christopher Wren	Louis Pasteur	Nelson Mandela
Simon Bolivar	Golda Meir	Madame Curie
Dwight D. Eisenhower	Eleanor Roosevelt	Mother Theresa
Robert Redford	George Clooney	Meryl Streep
Richard Gere	Bart Simpson	George Harrison

Newspapers

New York Times	Philadelphia Inquirer	The Baltimore Sun
Wall Street Journal	Daily News	Daily Record
Washington Post	USA Today	Boston Globe

Schools

Harvard University	University of Maryland	Johns Hopkins University
University of Michigan	Boston University	Northeastern University
Columbia University	Berklee School of Music	Boston College
Perkins School for the Blind	Nassau Community College	Culinary Institute of America
New England Conservatory	Peabody Conservatory	Massachusetts College of Art

Add some proper nouns that you frequently use in your speech.

```
┌─────────────────────────────────────────────────────────────┐
│  Personal Word List                                         │
│                                                             │
│                                                             │
│                                                             │
│                                                             │
└─────────────────────────────────────────────────────────────┘
```

Exercise 2: Read the following sentences. Underline and stress the appropriate word, then read the sentence aloud.

CD
1:13

1. *The Pittsburgh Steelers and the Seattle Seahawks met in the 2006 Super Bowl.*

2. *We crossed the Atlantic Ocean to see the Eiffel Tower.*

3. *The Tower of London and Westminster Abbey are in Great Britain.*

4. *Lake Michigan is one of the Great Lakes.*

5. *We strolled down Fifth Avenue in New York City.*

6. Rodeo Drive is a famous shopping area in Los Angeles.

7. The Golden Gate Bridge is in San Francisco.

8. Mt. Rushmore is located in South Dakota.

9. We traveled to Costa Rica and El Salvador.

10. He was admitted to Johns Hopkins in Baltimore, Maryland.

11. The Smithsonian Institution and Lincoln Memorial are in Washington, D.C.

12. Cross the Chesapeake Bay Bridge to get to the Eastern Shore.

13. George Washington was the first president of the United States.

14. The Statue of Liberty is in the Hudson River.

15. New Orleans was devastated by Hurricane Katrina.

16. Las Vegas is famous for casinos and gambling.

17. New Zealand is in the Southern Hemisphere.

18. Could the Boston Red Sox have another chance at the World Series?

19. The National Gallery exhibits many paintings by Vincent Van Gogh.

20. Royal Caribbean and Holland America are two popular cruise lines.

21. Prince William's mother was Princess Diana.

22. Senator Kennedy is the senior senator from Massachusetts.

23. Sir Laurence Olivier was a well-respected actor.

24. Sir Anthony Hopkins was nominated for an Academy Award for his portrayal of Hannibal Lector in *Silence of the Lambs*.

25. Paul Newman and Joanne Woodward are a famous Hollywood couple.

5. Heteronym Pairs

CD
1:14

Heteronyms are words pairs that are spelled the same way (homographs) but differ by part of speech (noun/adjective vs. verb), word meaning, and pronunciation stress patterns.

Two syllable words*: If the word is a noun, the <u>first</u> syllable is stressed (higher, louder, longer), e.g.,* **con***tract. If the word is a verb, the <u>second</u> syllable is stressed, e.g.,* con***tract****.*

Three syllable words*: Both nouns and verbs stress the first syllable. The verbs have primary stress on the first syllable, secondary stress on the third syllable and weak stress on the second syllable, e.g.,* **grad***uate. Nouns or adjectives have primary stress on the first syllable, with short, unstressed second and third syllables, often changing the pronunciation of the last syllable, e.g.,* **grad***-u-it.*

Exercise 1: Read the sentences below and decide which stress pattern should be used for each sentence. Then say the sentence aloud.

CD
1:15

---

1.   **A. con***tract*   **B.** con***tract***

You need to sign the _____.

Wash your hands thoroughly so we don't _____ any illnesses.

---

2.   **A. con***flict*   **B.** con***flict***

I'm afraid my travel schedules will _____ with the training program.

I'm sorry; I can't meet you at 3:00 p.m. because I have a scheduling _____.

---

3.   **A. con***trast*   **B.** con***trast***

Let's compare and _____ the two options.

This decorating scheme is quite a _____ to her usual style.

---

4. **A. es**timate   **B. es**timate *(primary and secondary stress)*

We received a reasonable _____ for the car repair.

How long do you _____ it will take to complete?

---

5. **A. grad**uate   **B. grad**uate *(primary and secondary stress)*

When will you _____ from the University?

Where are you going for _____ school?

---

6. **A. aff**ect   **B. aff**ect

After a head injury or a stroke, a person's _____ can change.

How do you think the layoffs will _____ employee morale?

---

7. **A. pro**ject   **B. pro**ject

I hope to finish my _____ before the deadline.

It is so hard to _____ our anticipated sales figures.

---

8. **A. sub**ject   **B. sub**ject

Don't _____ him to so much pressure.

He was a _____ in the experiment.

6. Acronyms and Initializations

CD
1:16

Acronyms and initializations are shortcuts for frequently used words. The terms are frequently used interchangeably with "abbreviations." The word "initialization" is used in literature pertaining to second language learners. These abbreviated forms of a word or phrase usually consist of the single letters corresponding to each word of the term or phrase.

Acronyms are pronounced as a complete word, such as AMEX (American Express) or MADD (Mothers Against Drunk Driving). Acronyms are identified with an asterisk✱.

Abbreviations/Initializations are pronounced by saying each letter individually, e.g., M.D. (medical doctor), VP (Vice President). Formal abbreviations typically have periods after the letters, while informal ones are usually written without them.

*Lists of acronyms and initializations/abbreviations are exhaustive. Often, there are numerous meanings for one particular initialization or acronym. In this exercise, you may see the same notation under several headings because it is used to mean different things in different contexts. For example, **PI** may stand for **Personal Injury** to a lawyer, **Private Investigator** to a policeman, or **Principal Investigator** to a researcher.*

It is best to consult the internet or a special dictionary if you are unsure. Your frame of reference may differ from the most popular use.

*The primary stress is on the **last** letter of the abbreviation/ initialization, e.g., VP. An acronym is usually pronounced as **one word**, e.g., NASDAQ.*

Exercise 1: Read the following acronyms or initializations/abbreviations aloud and state what they represent. For example, "USA stands for the United States of America." Remember to read the items with an asterisk ✱ as a complete word vs. one letter at a time and read the initializations with stress on the last letter.

Key code:

✱	Say these as a complete word (acronym)
†	Say these either as a complete word _or_ one letter at a time
✖ ✖	Say these with the first letter, then the remainder as a complete word, e.g. "LSAT"

Academic Terms

B.A.	Bachelor of Arts	B.S.	Bachelor of Science
M.A.	Master of Arts	M.S.	Master of Science
MBA	Master in Business Administration	Ph.D.	Doctor of Philosophy
GED	General Education Diploma	M.S.W.	Masters in Social Work
PI	Principal Investigator	NYU	New York University
AA	Associate of Arts	CS	Computer Science
MIT	Massachusetts Institute of Technology	TA	Teaching Assistant
USC	University of Southern California	UNH	University of New Hampshire
BU	Boston University	BC	Boston College
UCLA	University of California Los Angeles	RPI	Rensselaer Polytechnic Institute
RSDI✷	Rhode Island School of Design	RIT	Rochester Institute of Technology
UVM	University of Vermont	SUNY✷	State University of New York
ESL	English as a Second Language	LEP	Limited English Proficient
ELL	English Language Learner	GRE	Graduate Record Examination
SAT	Standard Achievement Test	PSAT	Preliminary Scholastic Assessment Test
MCAT✗✗	Medical College Admission Test	LSAT✗✗	Law School Admission Test
GMAT✗✗	Graduate Management Admission Test	ESOL✗✗	English for Speakers of Other Languages

Medical/Healthcare Terms

M.D.	Medical Doctor	DO	Doctor of Osteopathy
PA	Physician's Assistant	URI	Upper Respiratory Infection
RN	Registered Nurse	LPN	Licensed Practical Nurse
HMO	Health Maintenance Organization	DDS	Doctor of Dental Surgery
AMA	American Medical Association/ Against Medical Advice	ER	Emergency Room

PT	*Physical Therapist*	SLP	Speech-Language Pathologist
CNA	*Certified Nursing Assistant*	PET✳	Positron Emission Tomography
MRI	*Magnetic Resonance Imaging*	CAT✳	Computerized Axial Tomography
CVA	*Cerebrovascular accident (stroke)*	TIA	Transient Ischemic Attack (mini-stroke)
DNA	*Deoxyribonucleic acid*	DOA	Dead on arrival
OT	*Occupational Therapist*	OR	Operating Room
LASER✳	*Light Amplification by Stimulated Emission of Radiation*	FDA	Food & Drug Administration
UTI	*Urinary Tract Infection*	MI	Myocardial Infarction
CAD	*Coronary Artery Disease*	DVT	Deep Vein Thrombosis
TBI	*Traumatic Brain Injury*	MVA	Motor Vehicle Accident
RNA	Ribonucleic Acid	DM	Diabetes Mellitus
OB/GYN	Obstetrician/Gynecologist	ENT	Ear, Nose and Throat Specialist
GP	General Practitioner	GI	Gastroenterologist
ADHD	Attention Deficit Hyperactivity Disorder	CBC	Complete Blood Count
IV	Intravenous	IM	Intramuscular
AAC	Augmentative and Alternative Communication	IVF	Invitro fertilization
HDL	High Density Lipoprotein	LDL	Low Density Lipoprotein

Business/Finance Terms

LLC	*Limited Liability Corporation*	DBA	Doing Business As
ATM	*Automated Teller Machine Bank*	MBO	Management Buy Out
IRA†	*Individual Retirement Account*	SEP✳	Simplified Employee Pension
CD	*Certificate of Deposit*	PER	Price Earnings Ratio

IRS	Internal Revenue Service	FRB	Federal Reserve Bank
FDIC	Federal Deposit Insurance Corporation	NYSE	New York Stock Exchange
SEC	Securities and Exchange Commission	TIN	Tax Identification Number
EIN	Employer Identification Number	PIN✱	Personal Identification Number
EPS	Earnings per Share	ROI	Return on Investments
EBIT✱	Earnings Before Interest and Tax	EVA	Economic Value Added
IT	Information Technology	IPO	Initial Public Offering
NASDAQ✱	National Association of Securities Dealers Automated Quotations	PR	Public Relations
AMEX✱	American Express	HP	Hewlett-Packard
IBM	International Business Machines	GE	General Electric

Mail/Shipping Terms

UPS	United Parcel Service	GDP	Gross Domestic Product
COD	Cash on Delivery	P.O.	Post Office
FOB	Freight on Board	PO	Purchase Order
FedEx	Federal Express		
	(pronounced as a compound noun **Fed**Ex)		

Computer/Electronic/ Communication Terms

http	hypertext transfer protocol	URL	Uniform Resource Locator
www	World Wide Web	SPAM✱	Short Pointless Annoying Messages
iPOD✗✗	Internet Phone Over Data	DSL	Digital Subscriber Line
LED	Light Emitting Diode	LCD	Liquid Crystal Display
PC	Personal Computer	IBM	International Business Machine
LAN✱	Local Area Network	WAN✱	Wide Area Network
AOL	America On Line	WIFI✱	Wireless Fidelity
PDA	Personal Digital Assistant	DVD	Digital Video Disc

VCR	Videocassette Recorder	TV	Television
CD	Compact Disc	RW	Read, Write
VHF	Very High Frequency	DSL	Digital Subscriber Line/ Dedicated System Line
IT	Information Technology	OO	Object Oriented
BIOS*	Basic Input/Output System	DOS*	Disk Operating System
SCSI*	Small Computer System Interface	NAS*	Network Attached Storage
RAM*	Random Access Memory	CAD*	Computer Aided Design
SAN*	Storage Area Network	DVT	Design Verification Test
CPU	Central Processing Unit	USB	Universal Serial Bus
OEM	Original Equipment Manufacturer		

Mass Communication Terms

CNN	*Cable News Network*	TNT	Turner Network Television
NPR	*National Public Radio*	BBC	British Broadcasting Company
ESPN	*Entertainment and Sports Programming*	CBS	Columbia Broadcasting System
ABC	*American Broadcasting Corporation*	HBO	Home Box Office
PBS	*Public Broadcasting System*	AP	Associated Press
CBC	*Canadian Broadcasting Corporation*	NBC	National Broadcasting Corporation

Occupations/Departments

DA	*District Attorney*	PI	Private Investigator
DJ	*Disc Jockey (exception **DJ**)*	VP †	Vice President
CFO	*Chief Financial Officer*	COO	Chief Operating Officer
CEO	*Chief Executive Officer*	HR	Human Resources
CPA	*Certified Public Accountant*	HQ	Headquarters
QA	*Quality Assurance*	CTO	Chief Technology Officer
SVP	*Senior Vice President*	PM	Project Manager

Sports Terms

NBA	National Basketball Association	MLB	Major League Baseball
NFL	National Football League	NHL	National Hockey League
NCAA	National Collegiate Athletic Association	WWF	World Wrestling Federation
PGA	Professional Golf Association	TKO	Technical Knock Out
USTA	United States Tennis Association	RBI	Runs Batted In
ERA	Earned Run Average	NASCAR*	National Association for Stock Car Auto Racing
ACC	Atlantic Coast Conference		

Organizations

AAA	American Automobile Association	NRA	National Rifle Association
ASPCA	American Society for the Prevention of Cruelty to Animals	SWAT*	Special Weapons Action Team
PTA	Parent/Teacher Association	UNICEF*	United Nations International Children's Emergency Fund
AARP	American Association of Retired Persons	AA	Alcoholic Anonymous
UN	United Nations	USA	United States of America
CIA	Central Intelligence Agency	EU	European Union
FBI	Federal Bureau of Investigation	SADD*	Students Against Destructive Decisions
MADD*	Mothers Against Drunk Driving	NASA*	National Aeronautics and Space Administration
NATO*	North Atlantic Treaty Organization	UNESCO*	United Nations Educational, Scientific and Cultural Organization
OPEC*	Organization of Petroleum Exporting Countries	NYPD	New York Police Department
NYFD	New York Fire Department	LAPD	Los Angeles Police Department

EPA	Environmental Protection Agency	USCIS	United States Citizenship & Immigration Services

Transportation Terms

NOTE: The transit systems, public transportation, and airports frequently use abbreviations and acronyms.

DMV	Department of Motor Vehicles	MBTA	Mass Bay Transit Authority
BART*	Bay Area Rapid Transit	SEPTA	Southeast Pennsylvania Transportation Authority
MTA	Maryland Transit Authority	IRT	Interborough Rapid Transit
BMT	Brooklyn Manhattan Transit	LIE	Long Island Expressway
BQE	Brooklyn-Queens Expressway	LAX	Los Angeles Airport
JFK	John F. Kennedy Airport	BWI	Baltimore-Washington International Airport
SUV	Sports Utility Vehicle	RV	Recreational Vehicle
BMW	Bavarian Motor Works	VW	Volkswagen
ETA	Estimated Time of Arrival		

Text Messaging/E-Mail Terms

IMO	In My Opinion	COB	Close of Business
MYOB	Mind Your Own Business	LOL	Laughing Out Loud
BRB	Be Right Back	BLOG*	Web Log
ASAP**	As Soon As Possible	Cc	Carbon copy
BCC	Blind carbon copy	FYI	For Your Information

Countries & Cities

USA	United States of America	PRC	People's Republic of China
UN	United Nations	DC	District of Columbia

| LA | Los Angeles | BC | British Columbia |

Miscellaneous Terms

IOU	I Owe You	IQ	Intelligence Quotient
MIA	Missing in Action	POW	Prisoner of War
PSA	Public Service Announcement	TGIF	Thank Goodness It's Friday
BYOB	Bring Your Own Booze/Beer	TLC	Tender Loving Care
KISS✱	Keep It Simple Stupid	PDA	Public Display of Affection
O.K.	Okay	PA	Public Announcement
SNAFU✱	Situation Normal All Fouled Up	ID	Identification
VIP	Very Important Person	AWOL✖✖	Absent Without Leave
PC	Politically Correct	AKA	Also Known As
TBA	To Be Announced/To Be Arranged	P.S.	Post Script
Q & A	Questions and Answers	RSVP	Répondez S'il Vous Plaît (please respond)
FAQ	Frequently Asked Questions	GOP	Grand Old Party

Key code:
✱	Say these as a complete word (acronym)
†	Say these either as a complete word _or_ one letter at a time
✖✖	Say these with the first letter, then the remainder as a complete word, e.g. "LSAT"

Exercise 2: Now list acronyms and initializations that relate to your profession or geographic location. For example, think of the call letters for your local television affiliates or radio stations, local colleges and/or specialty schools, healthcare plans, sports clubs, transit systems, utility company, and businesses.

For instance, someone in Boston may attend **BC** (Boston College), be a member of the **BCC** (Brookline Chamber of Commerce), work out at the **BSC** (Boston Sports Club), listen to radio station **CRB** (Classical Radio of Boston), and get medical coverage through **HPHC** (Harvard Pilgrim Healthcare). Although a "local" would be familiar with these initializations/abbreviations and acronyms, someone who lives outside of the area may not.

Personal acronyms and initializations/abbreviations:

Exercise 3: Every work setting has its own corporate culture and vocabulary. Make a list of the many acronyms and initializations/abbreviations specific to your workplace. Practice saying them aloud and make up sentences to practice the correct pronunciation. Remember to stress the last letter of the initialization/abbreviation.

Work-related acronyms and initializations/abbreviations:

> **NOTE:** Some initializations/abbreviations, particularly in the medical field, are written with or without periods.

CD 1:18

Exercise 4: Practice reading aloud the following sentences using the appropriate stress on the acronym or last initial of the initialization/abbreviation.

1. *Is the program on ABC or HBO?*

2. *He received his B.A. and M.S. from UCLA.*

3. *RSVP to the party and remember it's BYOB.*

4. *The conference was filled with RNs and LPNs.*

5. *The CEO and CFO are on the Executive Board of that organization.*

6. Please reply to the memo from HR ASAP.

7. The VIPs waited in the Green Room before their appearance on NBC.

8. There are thirteen MDs affiliated with that HMO.

9. Insert the CD in your PC or laptop.

10. I studied for my Ph.D. in the USA.

11. After receiving his M.B.A., he formed an LLC with his business partner.

12. As the price of gas rises, it's advisable to sell your SUV ASAP.

13. Send the PSA to the PR Department of ABC News.

14. Sam Smith, AKA "the motivator," was an excellent team leader.

15. He received a list of FAQs prior to the press conference.

16. His notice from the IT Department is FYI.

17. The patient left the hospital AMA and returned to the ER that evening.

18. The DA presented DNA evidence found at the crime scene.

19. I often listen to the BBC on NPR.

20. The UN Security Council spokesperson was interviewed on CNN.

21. The SWAT officers showed up at the hostage situation.

22. NASA cancelled the mission due to a SNAFU.

23. We installed a DVD player in our new SUV.

24. At the end of the letter, she wrote "P.S. I love you."

25. The students did a fundraiser for MADD and SADD.

26. Don't forget your PIN when you go to the ATM.

27. Please tape the NBC special on your VCR.

28. Which NFL team will be televised on ESPN?

29. Mikel couldn't decide if he should invest his money in an IRA or a SEP.

30. Mariel read the Wall Street Journal for an update on the NASDAQ and the NYSE.

31. Richard drove across the U.S. from DC to LA.

32. Lam was stuck in traffic on the BQE and the LIE.

33. The Red Sox fan memorized the RBIs of the players.

Exercise 5: Look at the map of the United States of America. Write the complete names of each of the states for the following abbreviations. Practice reading the entire sentence aloud. Remember to stress the last letter of the abbreviation.

THE UNITED STATES OF AMERICA

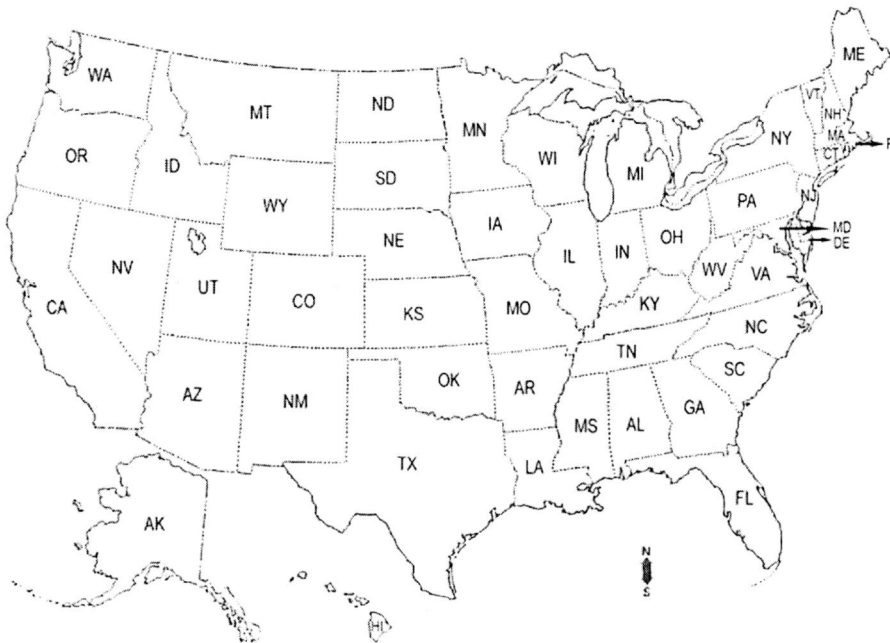

1. AL is the abbreviation for _____.

2. AK is the abbreviation for _____.

3. AR is the abbreviation for _____.

4. AZ is the abbreviation for _____.

5. CA is the abbreviation for _____.

6. CO is the abbreviation for _____.

7. CT is the abbreviation for _____.

8. DE is the abbreviation for _____.

9. FL is the abbreviation for _____.

10. GA is the abbreviation for _____.

11. HI is the abbreviation for _____.

12. ID is the abbreviation for _____.

13. IL is the abbreviation for _____.

14. IN is the abbreviation for _____.

15. IA is the abbreviation for _____.

16. KS is the abbreviation for _____.

17. KY is the abbreviation for _____.

18. LA is the abbreviation for _____.

19. ME is the abbreviation for _____.

20. MD is the abbreviation for _____.

21. MA is the abbreviation for _____.

22. MI is the abbreviation for _____.

23. MN is the abbreviation for _____.

24. MO is the abbreviation for _____.

25. MS is the abbreviation for _____.

26. MT is the abbreviation for _____.

27. NE is the abbreviation for _____.

28. NV is the abbreviation for _____.

29. NH is the abbreviation for _____.

30. NJ is the abbreviation for _____.

31. NM is the abbreviation for _____.

32. NY is the abbreviation for _____.

33. NC is the abbreviation for _____.

34. ND is the abbreviation for _____.

35. OH is the abbreviation for _____.

36. OK is the abbreviation for _____.

37. OR is the abbreviation for _____.

38. PA is the abbreviation for _____.

39. RI is the abbreviation for _____.

40. SC is the abbreviation for _____.

41. SD is the abbreviation for _____.

42. TN is the abbreviation for _____.

43. TX is the abbreviation for _____.

44. UT is the abbreviation for _____.

45. VT is the abbreviation for _____.

46. VA is the abbreviation for _____.

47. WA is the abbreviation for _____.

48. DC is the abbreviation for _____.

49. WV is the abbreviation for _____.

50. WI is the abbreviation for _____.

51. WY is the abbreviation for _____.

NOTE: To help pronounce the states, the International Phonetic Alphabet (IPA) is used. There are regional preferences in the pronunciation of states. Please defer to the local dialect.

Answers

CD
2:1

NOTE: The stressed syllable is in bold letters.

1. *Alabama*   [æləbæmə]
2. *Alaska*   [əlæskə]
3. *Arkansas*   [arkænsɔ]
4. *Arizona*   [ærəzonə]
5. *California*   [kæləfɔrnjə]
6. *Colorado*   [kalərado]
7. *Connecticut*   [kənɛtəkət]
8. *Delaware*   [dɛləwer]
9. *Florida*   [flarɪdə] [flɔrɪdə]
10. *Georgia*   [dʒɔrdʒə]
11. *Hawaii*   [həwaɪi]
12. *Idaho*   [aɪdəho]
13. *Illinois*   [ɪlənɔɪ]
14. *Indiana*   [ɪndiænə]
15. *Iowa*   [aɪowə]
16. *Kansas*   [kænzəs]
17. *Kentucky*   [kəntʌki]
18. *Louisiana*   [ləwiziænə]
19. *Maine*   [meɪn]
20. *Maryland*   [mɛrələnd]
21. *Massachusetts* [mæsətʃusəts]
22. *Michigan*   [mɪʃəgən]
23. *Minnesota*   [mɪnəsotə]
24. *Missouri*   [mɪzɔri]
25. *Mississippi*   [mɪsɪsɪpi]

26. *Montana*	[mɑntænə]
27. *Nebraska*	[nəbræskə]
28. *Nevada*	[nəvɑdə]
29. *New Hampshire*	[nu **hæm**ʃər]
30. *New Jersey*	[nu **ʤɝ**zi]
31. *New Mexico*	[nu **mɛk**səko]
32. *New York*	[nu **jɔrk**]
33. *North* Carolina	[nɔrθ kærəlaɪnə]
34. *North Dakota*	[nɔrθ dəkodə]
35. *Ohio*	[ohaɪo]
36. *Oklahoma*	[okləhomə]
37. *Oregon*	[ɔrəgən]
38. *Pennsylvania*	[pɛnsəlveɪnjə]
39. *Rhode Island*	[rod aɪlənd]
40. *South Carolina*	[saʊθ kærəlaɪnə]
41. *South Dakota*	[saʊθ dəkodə]
42. *Tennessee*	[tɛnəsi]
43. *Texas*	[tɛksəs]
44. *Utah*	[jutɑ]
45. *Vermont*	[vɝmɑnt]
46. *Virginia*	[vɝʤɪnjə]
47. *Washington*	[waʃɪŋtən]
48. *Washington, DC*	[waʃɪŋtən disi]
49. *West Virginia*	[wɛst vɝʤɪnjə]
50. *Wisconsin*	[wɪskɑnsən]
51. *Wyoming*	[waɪomɪŋ]

7. Syllable Stress Patterns

Although there may be exceptions, most words will follow these rules. As words increase in length, sometimes the syllables become reduced and this alters the stress pattern.

First, you must be able to determine how to divide the word into syllables.

Follow these guidelines to divide a word into syllables:

A syllable is one or more letters representing a unit of spoken language. Every syllable must contain at least <u>one</u> vowel (V). It can be a vowel alone or a combination of one or more consonants (C) and a vowel. It will have only one vowel sound. Sometimes two vowels may make up one sound, e.g., ai, ay, ee, ea, oa, ow.
NOTE: Although /w/ is a semi-vowel or glide, it has been included in this group.

    e-lec-tric   **a-lone**   **sea-son**   **meet-ing**

With an open syllable (CV), you pronounce the vowel's "name," e.g., (A, E, I, O, U). With a closed syllable (CVC), you pronounce the "sound" of the vowel, e.g., [æ, ɛ, ɪ, ɑ, ʌ, ə] or (a, eh, ih, ah, uh). With two vowels in a closed syllable, you may pronounce the "name" of the vowel ("meeting"). This rule will help you pronounce unfamiliar syllables.

	CV	CV
Open syllable (CV)	**ta-ble**	**cli-ent**

	CVC	CVC CVC
Closed syllable (CVC)	**sub-way**	**pen-cil**

1. In a VCCV pattern, divide it between the two consonants, unless they are a blend.

VC/CV	VC/CV	VCC / V
win/dow	**bot/tom**	**wash/er**

2. In a VCV pattern, divide it after the first vowel.

V / CV   V / CV

stu/dent   **re/port**

3. Sometimes a VCV pattern is divided after the consonant.

VC / V   VC / V

lim / it   **sec / ond**

4. When you have three consonants together in the VCCCV pattern, you <u>usually</u> divide the word after the first consonant. If it does not sound correct you can then divide it after the second consonant. We <u>usually</u> keep consonant blends together, e.g., br, pr, tr, dr, cr, gr, fr, sp, st, sk, spr, str, bl, pl, cl, gl, fl, sl, spl, th, sh, and ch.

VC/ CCV   VC/ CCV

con/tract   **sur/prise**

NOTE: It is often difficult to determine how to divide a word into syllables. Consult a dictionary if you are unsure.

5. Prefixes and suffixes form separate syllables.

re/write   **care/ful**

Rules for Syllable Stress

NOTE: For the following rule, the suffix may have more than one syllable and it may not be divided at the exact syllable juncture. For the purpose of this exercise, the suffix is separated as one unit, rather than by a syllable.

1. Give primary stress to the syllable before the following suffixes: -**ic**, -**ical**, -**ify**, -**omy**, -**ogy**, -**edy**, -**istry**, -**metry**, -**ive**, -**ity**, -**tion**, -**ion**, -**ious**, -**ily**, -**eous**, -**able**, -**ible**, -**ophy**, -**graphy**, -**ogist**, -**cian**

NOTE: Due to syllable rules, a consonant may be at the beginning of the suffix, e.g., coILEC<u>tible</u>.

Exceptions: **com**fortable, **veg**etable, **irr**itable, **form**idable, com**pet**itive, con**sec**utive, ma**nip**ulative

doMEStic   *eco<u>NOM</u>ical*   *<u>CHEM</u>ical*   *i<u>DEN</u>tify*

CD
2:2

SPEC<u>i</u>fy	_e<u>LEC</u>trify_	_e<u>CON</u>omy_	_au<u>TON</u>omy_
bi<u>OL</u>ogy	_<u>COM</u>edy_	_<u>CHEM</u>istry_	_trigo<u>NOM</u>etry_
ob<u>JECT</u>ive	_elec<u>TRI</u>city_	_cre<u>A</u>tion_	_pro<u>GRES</u>sion_
sus<u>PI</u>cion	_<u>CON</u>scious_	_consci<u>EN</u>tious_	_momen<u>TAR</u>ily_
tempo<u>RAR</u>ily	_cou<u>RA</u>geous_	_advan<u>TA</u>geous_	_de<u>PEN</u>dable_
in<u>TAN</u>gible	_phi<u>LOS</u>ophy_	_ge<u>O</u>graphy_	_psy<u>CHOL</u>ogist_
pedia<u>TRI</u>cian	_obste<u>TRI</u>cian_	_mathema<u>TI</u>cian_	_endocri<u>NOL</u>ogist_

CD
2:3

2. *Give primary stress to the syllable that is <u>ONE</u> syllable before the suffix -**meter**. Although we pronounce "-**meter**" with a long "e" [mitæ], when used as a suffix, the pronunciation changes to an unstressed vowel [mətæ].*

pe<u>DOM</u>eter	_ki<u>LOM</u>eter_	_spee<u>DOM</u>eter_
ba<u>ROM</u>eter	_ther<u>MOM</u>eter_	_o<u>DOM</u>eter_
pa<u>RAM</u>eter	_spi<u>ROM</u>eter_	_pen<u>TAM</u>eter_

Exercise 1: Say the following sentences and concentrate on the correct pronunciation of the suffix "-**meter**."

1. *Ilse uses a **<u>pedometer</u>** to measure her walking distance.*
2. *The **<u>barometer</u>** measures atmospheric pressure.*
3. *Keep checking the **<u>speedometer</u>** to make sure you drive within the speed limit.*
4. *Set the **<u>odometer</u>** so we know how much we drove this weekend.*
5. *Please pick up a new **<u>thermometer</u>** when you go to the drugstore.*
6. *Joanne writes poems in iambic **<u>pentameter</u>**.*
7. *Was that distance in miles or **<u>kilometers</u>**?*
8. *We need a **<u>spirometer</u>** to measure Lisa's lung capacity.*
9. *What **<u>parameters</u>** should we set for the results of our research?*
10. *A **<u>dynamometer</u>** is used to measure mechanical power.*

3. *Give primary stress to the syllable that is TWO syllables before the following suffixes: -ate, -ary (for three syllable words).*

However, when you have FOUR or MORE syllables, stress ONE syllable before the -ary suffix (elementary, exemplary, rudimentary).

NOTE: Suffixes may have more than one syllable.

Ap-*PRO*-pri-ate	*ES*-ti-mate	re-*FRIG*-er-ate
Ap-*PRE*-ci-ate	Ma-*NIP*-u-late	*CAL*-cu-late
ED-u-cate	*TEM*-por-ary	*CEM*-e-tary
VOL-un-tary	*SED*-en-tary	*OR*-di-nary

Unusual Circumstances

Typically prefixes are not stressed. However, when using a prefix to contradict a previous statement, stress the prefix. For example,

"Do you give presentations frequently?"

*"No, I give presentations **in**frequently."*

Exercise 2: First identify and underline the suffix. Then, underline the syllable that should receive the primary stress. Finally, say the word aloud.

tragic	auspicious	autonomy	psychology
expression	illogical	simplistic	university
autobiography	fantastic	maladaptive	theatrical
temporarily	logic	taxonomy	superstitious
trigonometry	elastic	expendable	ammunition
neonatology	geography	gorgeous	transliteration
unfortunate	chemistry	cosmic	constructive
terminology	conscientious	diversity	characteristic
cortical	anticipation	compatible	anticipate
ambitious	aggravation	magical	philosophy

©2006, RULES

defendable	anthropology	exemplary	parapsychologist
returnable	fortunately	superstition	mitigate
futuristic	philosophical	geometry	ordinarily
culinary	courageous	portable	immaculate
articulate	irritate	sedentary	ordinary
pathologist	political	reliable	competitive
delegate	orthopedic	designate	consecutive
rectify	convertible	contagious	prosperity

Occupations

There are some suffixes that are frequently used when referring to occupations. In the medical field, common suffixes include -**cian**, -**ist**, -**ologist**, and -**or**. Some of the following rules will help use the appropriate stress pattern when saying these multisyllable words.

---

4. *Give primary stress to the syllable that comes ONE syllable before -**cian**:*

phySIcian	*obsteTRIcian*	*geriaTRIcian*
pediaTRIcian	*opTIcian*	*dieTIcian*

---

5. *Give primary stress to the syllable that comes ONE syllable before -**ogist** or TWO syllables before -**ist**:*

rheumaTOLogist	*hemaTOLogist*	*onCOLogist*
psyCHOLogist	*dermaTOLogist*	*audiOLogist*
speech paTHOLogist	*gyneCOLogist*	*neuROLogist*
endocriNOLogist	*gastroenteROLogist*	*ophthalMOLogist*
neuropsyCHOLogist	*pulmoNOLogist*	*cardiOLogist*
phySIatrist	*psyCHIatrist*	*poDIatrist*
THERapist	*ALlergist*	*AcuPUNCturist*
JOURnalist		

Exceptions: perioDONtist, DENtist, orthoDONtist, inTERNist, orthoPEDist

6. *Give primary stress to the syllable before* **-man** *and treat it like a compound word. Stress the first part of the word. The suffix is sometimes unstressed and may sound like* [mən].

SALESman   FIREman   MAILman

POSTman   DOORman   CHAIRman

Exceptions: When you add **-man** *to a verb or noun to make it an occupation, do not alter the stress pattern of the root word; for example, PoLICEman, GARbageman, ANchorman.*

---

7. When you add **-er** or **-or** to a verb or noun to make it an occupation, do not alter the *stress pattern of the root word.*

TEACHer	BAKer	PAINTer
COUNselor	LAWyer	BROKer
deSIGNer	CONtractor	proFESsor
SINGer	DANCer	enterTAINer
PLUMBer	inTERrogator	rePORTer
adMINistrator	CAterer	inVEStigator

Exception: phoTOgrapher

Do <u>not</u> alter the stressed syllable when the suffix **–ing** is added. Stress <u>is</u> shifted when the suffix **–tion** is added.

locate	locating	location
estimate	estimating	estimation
calculate	calculating	calculation
appreciate	appreciating	appreciation
interrogate	interrogating	interrogation
administrate	administrating	administration
anticipate	anticipating	anticipation

Common Suffixes

Exercise 3: Collect some words in your daily vocabulary that have suffixes and include them in this list. Circle the suffix and try to say the word with the correct stress pattern. Use the rules that are listed earlier in this unit. Make up sentences with your **personal words**.

psychology	geology	meteorology
cosmetology	archeology	paleontology
geography	photography	calligraphy
communication	transportation	situation
construction	instruction	fabrication
expectation	anticipation	illustration

Personal Words

Medical Procedures

8. Many medical procedures have multiple syllables and are often difficult to pronounce. The syllable stress rules will help you determine which syllable to stress in the following procedures.

colon_OS_copy	en_DOS_copy	fiberoptic laryn_GOS_copy
trache_OT_omy	appen_DEC_tomy	_BI_opsy
tonsil_LEC_tomy	adenoi_DEC_tomy	co_LOS_tomy
hyste_REC_tomy	carotid endarter_EC_tomy	mas_TEC_tomy

Exercise 4: Read the above words aloud and concentrate on stressing the proper syllable. Make up some of your own sentences and practice your stress patterns.

Exercise 5: Answer the following questions and stress the appropriate syllable. Remember to use the rules for syllable stress and initializations/abbreviations.

1. If your feet were hurting, whom would you see? _____

2. If your baby had a high fever, which doctor would you see? _____

3. If you fell off your bicycle and had a concussion, whom would you see? _____

4. If your toddler had chronic ear infections, whom would you see? _____

5. If you needed to have a hip replacement, whom would you see? _____

6. If your elderly parent needed a new doctor, you might see a _____

7. If you had chronic arthritis, whom would you see? _____

8. If you needed to have a skin tag removed or had blemishes, whom would you see?

   _____

9. If one were pregnant, whom would she see? _____

10. If you were having vision problems, whom would you see? _____

11. If you needed radiation and chemotherapy, whom would you see? _____

12. If you broke out or had hives when you ate nuts, whom would you see? _____

13. If you needed to have your wisdom teeth extracted, whom would you see?_____

14. If your child needed braces, whom would you see? _____

15. If you were having reflux after eating, whom would you see? _____

16. If you were in rehabilitation for a hand injury, whom would you see? _____

17. If you were having flashbacks from Vietnam, whom would you see? _____

18. If you wanted to use Eastern Medicine for your migraines, whom would you see?

   _____

19. If you needed a check-up for general health, whom would you see? _____

20. If you needed to have sedation for surgery, whom would you see? _____

21. If your son had a stuttering problem, whom would you see?

   _____

22. If you were having heart palpitations, whom would you see? _____

23. If you suffered a mild head injury, whom would you see? _____

24. If you had a chronic lung condition, whom would you see? _____

25. If you needed an x-ray of a broken arm, whom would you see? _____

26. If you needed therapy to recover from a knee injury, whom would you see?

   _____

27. If you had emotional problems, whom would you see? _____

28. If you had back pain, one doctor you could see would be a _____

8. Sentence Level Stress Patterns

CD 2:5

Stress the last important word in a sentence. These words are nouns, verbs, adjectives, and adverbs and will rarely be pronouns, unless contrastive stress is needed. Contrastive stress is typically used to make our speech more emphatic, such as when strongly expressing a point or negating a comment.

> *It doesn't **work** for me. (typical pattern)*
>
> *It doesn't work for **me**. (contrastive stress; used for emphasis)*
>
> *It does **not** work for me. (contrastive stress; used for negation)*

NOTE: *Two people may not read a sentence the same way. The stressed words help communicate the intent and meaning.*

Keep the following guidelines in mind:

- *We tend to stress the last important word in a sentence that carries <u>new</u> information.*

    > *We'll discuss it at the **meeting**.*
    >
    > *We'll discuss it at the **Director's** meeting.*

- *We <u>usually</u> stress nouns, verbs, adjectives, adverbs (always, never, sometimes, another, so, very, etc.) and negatives.*

    > *She **always** arrives on time.*
    >
    > *I **don't** think I'll finish it.*

- *We <u>don't</u> typically stress pronouns, articles, or prepositions, <u>unless</u> we are emphasizing a particular word to clarify meaning.*

    > *No, please give the book to **me,** not to **him**.*
    >
    > *It is **on** the table, not **under** the table.*

- *Extremes of stress will affect the clarity and effectiveness of the message. You should stress at least <u>one</u> word in a thought group.*

NOTE: *Minimal use of stress will sound boring, flat, and disinterested. Excess use of stress will sound unnatural and awkward.*

- *Don't* stress two words next to each other.

    You can say:

    *"It is very **nice**,"   or   "It is **very** nice,"   but not,   "It is **very nice**."*

- *We speed up on words that are not stressed.*

- *We stress a word by saying it with a <u>higher</u> pitch, <u>louder</u> volume, and a <u>longer</u> key vowel sound.*

NOTE: *When the stressed word at the end of the sentence is a compound word, stress the first part of the compound word. For example, We must get a new **fire** extinguisher.*

Exercise 1: Say the following sentences focusing on the typical North American sentence stress pattern. First, read it with the typical pattern stressing the last <u>important</u> word. Then, read it again stressing the last word. Compare the two patterns. Remember to stress the word with a <u>higher</u> pitch, <u>louder</u> volume, and a <u>longer</u> key vowel sound.

NOTE: The word that is typically stressed is in bold.

CD 2:6

1. *I bought a special **gift** for you.*

2. *Jeff reserved **many** of them.*

3. *Shelley gave a **book** to her.*

4. *Jake ordered a **manual** for him.*

5. *Nikki sent the **package** to us.*

6. *Jayden wants to **speak** with her.*

7. *It looks really **nice** on you.*

8. *I need to **thank** him.*

9. *I watched that movie a long **time** ago.*

10. *Do you want to go to the **park** with me?*

11. Should I send the **results** to him?

12. He didn't want to **do** that.

13. What time are you going to **be** there?

14. I've had **enough** of that.

15. Let's **forget** about it.

16. Don't **worry** about it.

17. It doesn't **work** for me.

18. What will **help** me?

19. What can we **do** about it?

20. Jeff wants to **meet** with her.

Exercise 2: Read the same sentences without relying on any cues with bold type. First, underline the stressed word and then say it aloud. Compare <u>your</u> stressed word with the stressed word in Exercise 1.

CD
2:6

1. *I bought a special gift for you.*

2. *Jeff reserved many of them.*

3. *Shelley gave a book to her.*

4. *Jake ordered a manual for him.*

5. *Nikki sent the package to us.*

6. *Jayden wants to speak with her.*

7. *It looks really nice on you.*

8. *I need to thank him.*

9. *I watched that movie a long time ago.*

10. *Do you want to go to the park with me?*

11. Should I send the results to him?

12. He didn't want to do that.

13. What time are you going to be there?

14. I've had enough of that.

15. Let's forget about it.

16. Don't worry about it.

17. It doesn't work for me.

18. What will help me?

19. What can we do about it?

20. Jeff wants to meet with her.

Contrasting Word Stress in Sentences

When stressing words for emphasis within a sentence, keep in mind the general rule of higher, louder, and longer. This means that whatever word you are stressing needs to be spoken with <u>higher</u> pitch, <u>louder</u> volume, and a <u>longer</u> key vowel sound.

Exercise 3: Read the following sentences aloud, first using a traditional sentence stress pattern. Next, read it again, stressing the underlined word. Notice how the meaning of the sentence changes depending upon which word you stress. The first one is done for you. A possible intended meaning is provided after each sentence in sentence 1.

    1. *I'd like to know what she is doing here.*

> **I'd** like to know what she is doing here. *(You may not be interested, but <u>I</u> am!)*
>
> I'd **like** to know what she is doing here. *(I am <u>interested</u> in finding out.)*
>
> I'd like to **know** what she is doing here. *(I want to find out the <u>reason</u>.)*
>
> I'd like to know what **she** is doing here. *(I was expecting <u>someone else</u>.)*
>
> I'd like to know what she is **doing** here. *(What is she <u>doing</u>?)*
>
> I'd like to know what she is doing **here**. *(She was supposed to be <u>somewhere else</u>.)*

    2. Where would you like to go out to eat?

> **Where** would you like to go out to eat?
>
> Where **would** you like to go out to eat?
>
> Where would **you** like to go out to eat?
>
> Where would you **like** to go out to eat?
>
> Where would you like to go out to **eat**?

3. I'll never understand this complicated economic theory.

> **I'll** never understand this complicated economic theory.
>
> I'll **never** understand this complicated economic theory.
>
> I'll never **understand** this complicated economic theory.
>
> I'll never understand **this** complicated economic theory.
>
> I'll never understand this **complicated** economic theory.
>
> I'll never understand this complicated **economic** theory.
>
> I'll never understand this complicated economic **theory**.

4. Can you read what is printed on this sign?

> Can **you** read what is printed on this sign?
>
> Can you **read** what is printed on this sign?
>
> Can you read what is **printed** on this sign?
>
> Can you read what is printed on **this** sign?
>
> Can you read what is printed on this **sign**?

5. Which car has an expired registration sticker?

> **Which** car has an expired registration sticker?
>
> Which **car** has an expired registration sticker?
>
> Which car **has** an expired registration sticker?
>
> Which car has an **expired** registration sticker?
>
> Which car has an expired **registration** sticker?
>
> Which car has an expired registration **sticker**?

9. Numbers

CD 2:8

*When counting, stress the <u>first</u> syllable in "**teen**" numbers, e.g., **thir**teen, **four**teen, **fif**teen, **six**teen, **sev**enteen, **eigh**teen, **nine**teen.*

*When counting, stress the <u>second</u> number for numbers above twenty, e.g., twenty-**one**, twenty-**two**, twenty-**three**, twenty-**four**, twenty-**five**, twenty-**six**, twenty-**seven**, twenty-**eight**, twenty-**nine**.*

Exercise 1: Practice saying these aloud.

CD 2:9

*Thirty-**one**, thirty-**two**, thirty-**three**, thirty-**four**, thirty-**five**, thirty-**six**, thirty-**seven**, thirty-**eight**, thirty-**nine***

Forty-**one**, forty-**two**, forty-**three**, forty-**four**, forty-**five**, forty-**six**, forty-**seven**, forty-**eight**, forty-**nine**

Fifty-**one**, fifty-**two**, fifty-**three**, fifty-**four**, fifty-**five**, fifty-**six**, fifty-**seven**, fifty-**eight**, fifty-**nine**

Sixty-**one**, sixty-**two**, sixty-**three**, sixty-**four**, sixty-**five**, sixty-**six**, sixty-**seven**, sixty-**eight**, sixty-**nine**

Seventy-**one**, seventy-**two**, seventy-**three**, seventy-**four**, seventy-**five**, seventy-**six**, seventy-**seven**, seventy-**eight**, seventy-**nine**

Eighty-**one**, eighty-**two**, eighty-**three**, eighty-**four**, eighty-**five**, eighty-**six**, eighty-**seven**, eighty-**eight**, eighty-**nine**

Ninety-**one**, ninety-**two**, ninety-**three**, ninety-**four**, ninety-**five**, ninety-**six**, ninety-**seven**, ninety-**eight**, ninety-**nine**

Try these without reading the written numbers:

13, 14, 15, 16, 17, 18, 19, 20, 21, 22, 23, 24, 25, 26, 27, 28, 29, 30...

When stating numbers, as in time, money, or amounts, stress the <u>last</u> part of the *"teen"* numbers:

thir**teen**, four**teen**, fif**teen**, six**teen**, seven**teen**, eigh**teen**, nine**teen**

8:15	2:14	7:13	3:15	2:14
$15	$14	$18	$.16	$.17

NOTE: When stating numbers as it relates to money (dollars, pounds, Euros, etc.) or measurements (pounds, ounces, kilograms, meters, feet, miles, kilometers, etc.), use the preceding rules for pronouncing the number. However, the primary stress shifts to the nouns and the numbers receive secondary stress. For example,

fifty **doll**ars	six<u>ty</u> **cents**	<u>thir</u>ty **pounds**	<u>nine</u>ty **Eur**os
fif<u>teen</u> **doll**ars	six<u>teen</u> **cents**	thir<u>teen</u> **pounds**	nine<u>teen</u> **Eur**os

---

When counting <u>or</u> referring to the *"ten"* numbers, stress the <u>first</u> syllable:

twenty	**thir**ty	**for**ty	**fif**ty
sixty	**sev**enty	**eigh**ty	**nine**ty

When stating numbers to tell time, stress the <u>first</u> part of the *"ten"* numbers. For example, 9:30 is said, "nine **thir**ty."

6:30	9:20	7:40	3:50	11:30

This is in contrast to the stress pattern for *"teen"* numbers. Stress the <u>last</u> part of the *"teen"* numbers. For example, 9:13 is said, "nine thir**teen**."

2:15	11:17	4:14	9:13	8:16

NOTE: The second part of the number is in bold to denote the emphasis on "teen."

When stating numbers other than ten numbers, stress the last part of the number, e.g., twenty-**five**, thirty-**two**, seven**teen**.

8:14   7:35   6:55   3:17   11:45

NOTE: When stating numbers as it relates to money (dollars, pounds, Euros, etc.) or measurements (pounds, ounces, kilograms, meters, feet, miles, kilometers, etc.), use the preceding rules for pronouncing the number. However, the primary stress shifts to the nouns and the numbers receive secondary stress, e.g., fif**teen** **dollars**, six**teen** **cents**, thir**teen** **pounds**, nine**teen** **Euros**.

Exercise 2: Read the following columns of numbers aloud and be sure to stress the numbers according to the rules:

8:13	8:30
2:15	2:50
3:14	3:40
$19	$90
$18	$80
15 mg	50 mg
$18.80	$30.13
$90.19	$14.40

Exercise 3: Read the following ordinal numbers aloud. Make sure to pronounce the final endings in these ordinal numbers.

1	first	11	eleventh	30	thirtieth
2	second	12	twelfth	40	fortieth
3	third	13	thirteenth	50	fiftieth
4	fourth	14	fourteenth	60	sixtieth
5	fifth	15	fifteenth	70	seventieth
6	sixth	16	sixteenth	80	eightieth
7	seventh	17	seventeenth	90	ninetieth
8	eighth	18	eighteenth	100	hundredth
9	ninth	19	nineteenth	1000	thousandth
10	tenth	20	twentieth		

10. Reflexive Pronouns

*For reflexive pronouns, stress the suffix -**self** or -**selves**.*

*my**self***	*your**self***	*him**self***
*her**self***	*it**self***	*our**selves***
*your**selves***	*them**selves***	

**CD
2:10**

Exercise 1: Write the correct reflexive pronoun in the sentences below. Read your answers aloud, stressing the last part of the word.

1.   That is a beautiful sweater that you're wearing.
        Thanks, I made it _____ .
        I didn't know that you knew how to knit.
        My grandmother taught me when I was little, and I picked it up again recently.

2.   Did you hire a babysitter for this evening?
        No. I think the twins are old enough to stay home by _____.
        I suppose you're right. They aren't babies anymore.
        No, they are all grown up!

3.   Are you sure Bob built this deck all by _____ .
        Yes, he's incredibly handy with power tools.
        I would never be able to do it _____; I would have to hire a contractor.
        Me too!

4.   I can't believe that you are going to travel to Europe by _____.
        It does seem sort of daring, but I am an adventurous person.
        I would be too frightened to do it by _____.
        People travel by _____ all of the time. It's a wonderful way
        to meet people from other countries.

5.   Please clean up your rooms!
        Would you please help us?
        I think you are capable of doing it all by _____.
        Okay, Mom. We'll do it by _____.

6.   Did Janie prepare this entire Thanksgiving dinner by _____?
        She did most of the cooking, but Russ helped too.
        That's good. Too bad a meal for sixteen people can't cook _____.
        That would be quite amazing. Until then, we'll have to do it _____.

11. Tips for Telephone Communication

**CD
2:11**

Since the listener cannot see you while speaking on the telephone, communication becomes more difficult. Remember to speak slowly and clearly and use the following guidelines:

- *When you state a telephone number, speak in thought groups and completely pronounce the endings of numbers. State the area code first and then the rest of the number. You can use an intonation pattern as follows:*

        ↗   ↗ ↗↘
        419-378-7210

  NOTE: The arrows indicate a slightly rising and falling pitch change as you say the numbers.

- *If you have a name that may be difficult to spell or has letters that may be easily confused over the telephone, spell out each letter with examples for the difficult ones. Use all names of people, animals, or countries, so the listener can have a frame of reference. If you mix categories, it can become confusing.*

    *"This is Lynda Wilner. W-I-L-N as in **Nancy**-E-R."*

- Say your telephone numbers two times during the message to make sure the listener completely understands.

- Be consistent by saying 'o' (the letter) or 'zero' in the same number; don't switch between the two.

- If there are three of the same numbers say, "9996" vs. "triple 9 -6."
  Likewise, it is easier to understand "2-7-1-9" than "twenty-seven nineteen."

- If possible, stand when speaking on the phone. You will sound more energetic and will have an easier time projecting your voice.

- Smile when speaking as this will have a positive effect on your intonation and vocal expressiveness.

- Visualize the person with whom you are speaking. Imagine that you are having a face-to-face conversation.

- If you are leaving a message for someone in a country other than the United States, remember to group the numbers according to the grouping pattern of that country. For example, someone from Central America would break up his/her phone number as follows: 502-3312-4567.

- If you work in customer service or tech support, you might want to write out a script so that you have the answers in front of you. However, make sure you use proper stress patterns, pausing, and clear pronunciation to make it sound more natural.

In the space below, write your own work, home, mobile, and fax number. Practice saying these numbers with the above guidelines.

Home:

Work:

Mobile/Cell Phone:

Fax:

Pronunciation Rules

12. Voicing and Syllable Length

**CD
2:12**

> A vowel is held <u>longer</u> before a voiced consonant than a voiceless consonant.
>
> | | | | |
> |---|---|---|---|
> | s<u>a</u>**d** | *(voiced)* | s**at** | *(voiceless)* |
> | d<u>u</u>**g** | *(voiced)* | d**uck** | *(voiceless)* |
>
> **NOTE**: Refer to the unit on the American Sound System for more detailed information.

Exercise 1: Circle the word that has the longer vowel. Then, say the words aloud and focus on the correct pronunciation.

**CD
2:13**

1. *prize*	*price*	11. tack	tag
2. *feed*	*feet*	12. rack	rag
3. *white*	*wide*	13. robe	rope
4. *lap*	*lab*	14. rip	rib
5. *cab*	*cap*	15. mop	mob
6. *bit*	*bid*	16. cub	cup
7. *simple*	*symbol*	17. five	fife
8. *write*	*ride*	18. fleas	fleece
9. *wet*	*wed*	19. life	live
10. *bead*	*beat*	20. lies	lice

Exercise 2: This exercise can be done with a partner. Select one of the questions and say it aloud. Your partner answers the question or responds to the statement with the appropriate response. Your partner's response will let you know if you are pronouncing the key word correctly. If you are doing this alone, record yourself as you read a sentence and the correct response. Then, read the alternate sentence and response. Listen to the recording and decide if each of the sentences sounds correct.

---

1. What's wrong with his pri<u>ce</u>?   What's wrong with his pri<u>ze</u>?

   A. It is $5 higher than last year.
   B. He didn't want the silver medal; he wanted the gold!

---

2. I need to put a new bi<u>d</u> on that horse.   I need to put a new bi<u>t</u> on that horse.

   A. Why? His old one seems perfectly fine.
   B. How much are you willing to spend to train him?

---

3. What's in his la<u>p</u>?   What's in his la<u>b</u>?

   A. He has a furry kitten.
   B. He has mice for scientific experiments.

---

4. I don't need a ca<u>b</u>.   I don't need a ca<u>p</u>.

   A. Won't your head be cold?
   B. Are you sure that you want to walk?

---

5. It's not very wi<u>de</u>.   It's not very whi<u>te</u>.

   A. Do you think there is room to pass through?
   B. It could use a new coat of paint.

©2006, RULES

13. Linking Words Together

CD
2:14

The endings of words are important in American English and they carry more grammatical information than the beginning of the word. However, if we exaggerate the pronunciation, the flow of speech may become disrupted. When words are linked together, the message flows smoothly and sounds more natural.

Linking <u>doesn't</u> occur at the ends of thought groups, punctuation, or sentences.

The /d/ sound is a particularly difficult sound to link. When a word ends in a /d/ sound, make sure to link the /d/ with the beginning of the next word, whether it is a consonant or vowel. Bring your tongue behind your upper teeth as if you are ready to make a /d/ sound, but do not release the /d/. Place your tongue in the correct position for the sound of the second word to make a smooth transition and avoid the extra syllable "duh" or [də].

Exercise 1: Practice saying the following words and sentences and concentrate on linking the words so you <u>cannot</u> hear an extra syllable "uh" or [ə] between the two words, e.g. Red‿Sox vs. Red-ə-Sox.

Pay attention to the linking notation (‿) between final /d/ sounds and the initial sound of the following word. Read the sentences aloud and focus on linking the words together. Then try to read the sentences that follow without any linking notation.

NOTE: A final "e" is silent in the words identified with an asterisk*.

1. Final /d/ + Consonant

CD
2:15

Link the words together and <u>don't</u> release the final /d/.

Red‿Sox	bad‿news	mud‿room	bed‿room
feed‿me	food‿bank	guide*‿book	good‿night
lead‿time	paid‿leave	paid‿vacation	road‿block
rude‿remarks*	wide*‿lanes	wood‿pile	board‿room

NOTE: A final "e" is silent in the words identified with an asterisk*.

Sentences

1. Ted‿received‿two tickets for exceeding the speed‿limit and‿not wearing a seat belt.
2. The children raised‿money by setting up a lemonade‿stand.
3. Proceed‿slowly as you drive through the construction area.
4. It was difficult to persuade‿them to remain for the entire lecture.
5. The gardener sprayed‿the insecticide, trimmed‿the shrubs, and spread‿mulch in the beds.
6. Please download‿the updates on the QuickBooks™ program.
7. Please upgrade‿my ticket to business class.
8. Don't forget to shred‿the documents to prevent identity theft.
9. I hate to be the one to spread‿bad‿news.
10. Fred‿collected canned‿goods for the food‿bank.

CD
2:16

2. Final /d/ + Vowel

Link the words together and <u>don't</u> release the final /d/. The final /d/ should be produced quickly, using <u>light</u> contact between the tip of the tongue and the alveolar ridge behind the upper front teeth. You should <u>not</u> hear a /də/ between the words.

wide*‿open	good‿evening	red‿apple	lead‿in
paid‿up	bad‿attitude	wild‿animal	good‿idea
fed‿up	need‿us	ride*‿over	hide*‿it
said‿everything	made*‿up	stood‿up	lied‿about

NOTE: A final "e" is silent in the words identified with an asterisk*.

Sentences

1. During an ice storm, you can easily skid‿across the highway.
2. The strict teacher said, (no link due to punctuation) "I forbid‿it!" when asked about bringing iPods™ to class.
3. Let's go to the park instead‿of the zoo.
4. Matt was so sad‿about the tragic news.

5. Next time let's buy flood‿insurance before the hurricane season.

6. Floyd‿enjoys fresh-brewed‿iced tea on hot summer afternoons.

7. Jenna joined‿a neighborhood‿organization to prevent crime.

8. Do you have good‿or bad‿information for me?

9. They need‿us to ride‿over and pick up the platters.

10. He stood‿up at the meeting and said‿everything that was relevant.

3. Final /t/ + Consonant

CD
2:17

Link the words together and <u>don't</u> release the final /t/.

complete‿*transaction*	meat‿grinder	edit‿text	fit‿together
sit‿down	transmit‿fax	eat‿dinner	ought‿to
duplicate‿*checks*	indicate*‿trends	market‿share	split‿stocks
light‿rain	product‿release	expert‿witness	note*‿pad

NOTE: A final "e" is silent in the words identified with an asterisk*.

Sentences

1. *We ought‿to order duplicate‿checks for our financial records.*

2. *The teacher told her students to sit‿down and take out their note‿pads.*

3. *What is the expected date of the new product‿release?*

4. *You can buy a meat‿grinder in a specialty food shop.*

5. *Are you ready to eat‿dinner now?*

6. The graph will indicate‿trends in our field of research.

7. The expert‿witness approached the bench.

8. I can't‿figure out‿how these jigsaw puzzle pieces fit‿together!

9. My company has 65% of the total market‿share for that‿particular product.

10. The weather forecast‿called for light‿rain today and tomorrow.

4. Final /t/ + Vowel

CD
2:18

> Link the final /t/ to the vowel and be careful not to release the /t/. The /t/ will become a
> flap /t/. It is said more quickly, less precisely, and with some voicing; for example,
> "a lot‿of."
>
> sit‿up   start‿up   what‿about   wait‿up
>
> eat‿out   not‿again   admit‿it   heat‿up
>
> seat‿available   fit‿in   scoot‿over   illustrate*‿it
>
> let‿it (go)   caught‿on   get‿up   shut‿off
>
> **NOTE**: A final "e" is silent in the words identified with an asterisk*.

Sentences

> 1. The nurse said, "Please sit‿up and have something to drink."
> 2. I can heat‿up leftovers or we could eat‿out tonight.
> 3. Can you scoot‿over and make some room for me at the table?
> 4. She wrote‿a book and I am going to illustrate‿it.
> 5. Admit‿it; you like the paint color, right?
> 6. Would you rather work for an established company or a start-‿up?
> 7. I don't want to fight‿anymore; just let‿it go.
> 8. There is one seat‿available at‿our poetry reading.
> 9. It seems like yoga has really caught‿on in this area.
> 10. Can you get‿up by yourself or do you need some help?

5. Other Voiceless Consonants + Vowel

CD
2:19

> Final voiceless sounds are not usually released. However, when they are before a
> vowel-initiated word, linking occurs to make the words flow smoothly. The intensity of
> the final voiceless sound is reduced when linked with a vowel, e.g. "look" vs. "look‿up."

> Remember to link the final consonant with the following vowel:
>
> math‿equation   look‿up   miss‿out   chief‿officer
>
> pick‿up   with‿ease   watch‿out   cash‿in

stress‿out	finish‿up	keep‿up	seep‿in
rip‿up	shape*‿up	ship‿out	laugh‿a lot

NOTE: A final "e" is silent in the words identified with an asterisk*.

Sentences

1. *Eric can do this* math‿*equation* with‿*ease.*
2. *My sister and I* laugh‿*a lot when we get together.*
3. *If we don't repair the* leak‿*in the basement, the water will continue to* seep‿*in.*
4. *E-mail is a great way to* keep‿*up with friends and family.*
5. *Why did you* rip‿*up this newspaper?*
6. I hope to finish‿up this project by the end of the day.
7. Watch‿out; that floor is very slippery.
8. Who is the new chief‿officer at the bank?
9. Don't stress‿out about the deadline.
10. Will you please pick‿up the kids after school?

CD
2:20

6. Voiced Fricatives + Vowel

Remember to link the final sound with the following vowel:

achieve*‿it	give*‿up	believe*‿in	approve*‿of
smooth‿as	breathe*‿in	writhe*‿around	bathe*‿after
days‿off	as‿is	his‿answer	choose*‿another
ears‿and	eyes‿and	cruise*‿around	surprise*‿us

NOTE: A final "e" is silent in the words identified with an asterisk*.

Sentences

1. *What are you planning to do on your* days‿*off?*
2. *Breathe‿in deeply and close your eyes.*
3. *Please don't* give‿*up now!*
4. *Do you* approve‿*of requiring the elderly to take a driving test after age seventy?*

5. *If I buy this damaged item as‿is, can you deduct anything from the price?*
6. The baby's skin was‿as smooth as silk.
7. The newlyweds will crui**se‿a**round the Caribbean for their honeymoon.
8. They wanted to surpri**se‿us** with a party at our home.
9. His‿answer was not what we expected.
10. Please choo**se‿a**nother color for the family room.

7. Vowel-to-Vowel Linking

CD
2:21

As you link these two vowels together, insert a "w" sound for the rounded vowels, e.g., [o], [u].

go‿in	*go‿on*	*hello‿everyone*	*go‿ahead*
no‿exit	*show‿us*	*you‿are*	*how‿is*

As you link these two vowels together, insert a "y" sound for the unrounded vowels, e.g., [i], [e].

she‿allowed	*be‿inclined*	*he‿offered*	*may‿I*
see‿everything	*be‿aware*	*we‿are*	*tee‿off*

Sentences

1. *Go‿ahead and sho**w‿us** the room for the reception.*
2. *H**e‿o**ffered his bedroom to the house guests.*
3. *She‿allowed the children to go‿on the field trip.*
4. *Nikki can see‿everything from the top of the mountain.*
5. *We‿are going to tee‿off at 7:30.*
6. *May‿I go‿into the building before the meeting?*
7. *Be‿aware of strangers who follo**w‿us**.*
8. *There was n**o‿e**xit to be found in the crowded lobby.*
9. *H**e‿o**ffered to meet with us at noon.*
10. *He would be‿inclined to finish before the deadline.*

8. R-colored Vowels + Vowels

CD
2:22

> *Remember to link the /r/ sound to the following vowel:*
>
> | | | | |
> |---|---|---|---|
> | *far‿away* | jar‿open | are*‿able | door‿open |
> | *aware*‿of* | for‿us | more*‿interest | pour‿it |
> | *tore*‿it* | wore*‿out | ear‿ache | dear‿old |
> | *fear‿of* | share*‿everything | hear‿of | peer‿in |
> | *rear‿admiral* | tear‿off | pair‿off | rare*‿emerald |
> | *stare*‿at* | fire*‿away | steer‿away | tire*‿of |
> | *near‿and far* | wear‿out | higher‿up | stir‿up |
> | *her‿eyes* | butter‿up | litter‿only | mother‿of |
>
> **NOTE**: A final "e" is silent in the words identified with an asterisk*.

Sentences

> 1. *The mother‿of six hoped she didn't wear‿out her welcome at her‿in-laws' house. Did you hear‿of a rare‿emerald costing over‿eight million dollars? It will stir‿up trouble if you put recyclable bottles in the litter‿only bins.*
> 2. *Please leave the back door‿open for‿us when you go out.*
> 3. *Can you get this jar‿open for me?*
> 4. Her‿eyes hurt from the sun's glare.
> 5. The rear‿admiral faced that reporter‿at the news briefing and told him to "fire‿away."
> 8. I know I shouldn't stare‿at them, but I can't help myself.
> 9. The baby needs medicine for her‿earache.
> 10. Tear‿off the tag on your dress before you wear‿it.

9. L + Vowels

CD
2:23

> *Remember to link the /l/ to the following vowel:*
>
> | | | | |
> |---|---|---|---|
> | *all‿over* | feel‿it | they'll‿offer | automobile*‿owner |
> | *peel‿it* | repeal‿order | fill‿in | pill‿organizer |
> | *pale*‿ale* | compel‿us | tell‿everyone | all‿inclusive |
> | *mall‿opening* | small‿offer | bowl‿over | roll‿around |
> | *central‿air conditioning* | | national‿anthem | |
>
> NOTE: A final "e" is silent in the words identified with an asterisk*.

Sentences

> 1. Central‿air conditioning means that you can have cool‿areas all‿over your house.
> 2. You have to peel‿it before you eat it!
> 3. Let's tell‿everyone our exciting news!
> 4. You can buy a pill‿organizer for your medications or vitamins.
> 5. I am a proud automobile‿owner.
> 6. There are a lot of activities planned at the new mall‿opening this Saturday.
> 7. John likes to brew his own pale‿ale.
> 8. What do you think would compel‿us to act?
> 9. We booked an all‿-inclusive weekend at a fabulous resort.
> 10. My dog likes to roll‿around in the yard and chase Frisbees™.

10. M + Vowels

CD
2:24

> *Remember to link the final /m/ with the following vowel:*
>
> | | | |
> |---|---|---|
> | *climb‿up* ("b" is silent) | team‿up | time*‿out |
> | *come*‿away* | daydream‿about | deem‿appropriate |
> | *aim‿at* | became*‿obsessed | maximum‿allowance |
> | *blame*‿others* | clam‿up | Mom‿owes |
> | *confirm‿appointments* | come*‿over | minimum‿amount |
> | *chime*‿in* | I'm‿alone | prime*‿example |
>
> NOTE: A final "e" is silent in the words identified with an asterisk*.

82 ©2006, RULES

Sentences

1. The coach called a *time-⌣out* to re-assess his team's strategy.
2. Is our *time⌣up* yet?
3. Mike likes to *daydream⌣about* becoming a college basketball coach.
4. The *minimum⌣amount* needed to open a CD was $5000.
5. I like to *confirm⌣appointments* one week ahead of time.
6. This report is a *prime⌣example* of what needs to be addressed.
7. Feel free to *chime⌣in* with your answers.
8. Let's *team⌣up* with *some⌣experienced* people who can help us.
9. The cat tried to *climb⌣up* on the sofa.
10. Make whatever contribution you *deem⌣appropriate*.

11. Nasal (m,n) Consonant + Nasal Consonant

Remember to link the same sounds together and say them only one time.

team⌣members	skim⌣milk	slim⌣man
blame⌣myself*	same*⌣mistakes	room⌣mate
begin⌣now	contain⌣nuts	telephone*⌣number
pine⌣needle*	between⌣neighbors	learn⌣new
extreme⌣makeover*	scream⌣madly	steam⌣machine

NOTE: A final "e" is silent in the words identified with an asterisk*.

Sentences

1. The *team⌣members* had lunch before the meeting.
2. Does that recipe *contain⌣nuts*?
3. Dylan keeps making the *same⌣mistakes* over and over again.
4. I *blame⌣myself* for not completing the forms on time.
5. I would rather drink *skim⌣milk* than whole milk.
6. Elise likes to *learn⌣new* skills to improve her performance.
7. If you walk barefoot, you may step on the *pine⌣needles*.

8. I will try to memorize Nate's telepho**ne**‿**n**umber.

9. Let's begi**n**‿**n**ow and we'll tell Gloria what she missed.

10. He used to be a sli**m**‿**m**an, but now he is robust.

12. N + Vowels

Remember to say the /n/ sound with the tongue tip up behind the front teeth and link it to the following vowel.

explain‿it	phone*‿in	between‿owners
clean‿up	machine*‿operated	seen‿around
teen‿angst	begin‿again	chin‿up
gin‿and (tonic)	ruin‿everything	spin‿out
complain‿about	grain‿of (rice)	vain‿attempt
rain‿out	retain‿optimism	sign‿off

NOTE: A final "e" is silent in the words identified with an asterisk*.

Sentences

1. *Marjorie's clients asked her to explai**n**‿**i**t to them.*

2. *You can pho**ne**‿**i**n your choices on some television programs.*

3. *Sheryl called customer service to complai**n**‿**a**bout the late fee.*

4. *A car can spi**n**‿**o**ut of control o**n**‿**i**cy roads.*

5. *A rainy day ca**n**‿**o**ften rui**n**‿**e**verything that was planned.*

6. After the unsuccessful results, let's begi**n**‿**a**gain.

7. That was a vai**n**‿**a**ttempt to reconcile their differences.

8. His mother said, "Chi**n**‿**u**p. Things could be worse."

9. At the end of the radio show, he liked to sig**n**‿**o**ff with a quote for the day.

10. The property had dramatic changes betwee**n**‿**o**wners.

13. ŋ ("-ng") + Vowels

Remember to produce the [ŋ] sound by lifting the back of the tongue and link it to the following vowel.

bring‿it	hang‿on	baking‿apples

©2006, RULES

bring‿us	climbing‿up	confusing‿article
finding‿out	frying‿eggs	opening‿act
among‿us	morning‿after	criticizing‿enemies
feeding‿everyone	protecting‿environments	reversing‿attitudes
stinging‿insects	balancing‿accounts	sorting‿out

Sentences

1. *Hurry up; the opening‿act is about to begin!*
2. *We don't mind feeding‿everyone, as long‿as people don't mind helping‿us with the clean-up!*
3. *My mother is afraid of stinging‿insects.*
4. *The wedding‿is in the evening‿and a farewell brunch is scheduled for the morning‿after.*
5. *How many among‿us have ever tried rock climbing?*
6. I thought that was a very confusing‿article.
7. I was planning‿on spending the morning baking‿apples for the dinner party.
8. We've been sorting‿out our differences in counseling.
9. Can you bring‿us some literature on protecting‿environments?
10. Janie is online finding‿out about upcoming‿events at the beach.

CD
2:28

14. Fricatives (/s/, /z/, /f/, /v/, "sh" or /ʃ/, "th" or /θ,ð/) + Fricatives

Remember to link the same sounds together and say them only one time.

ice‿storm*	obese*‿sister	police*‿surveillance
space‿saver*	dress‿size	express‿service
waitress‿served	reduce*‿symptoms	nurse*‿supervisor
continuous‿siren	enormous‿sale	choice*‿setting
glorious‿sunshine	bus‿sign	dangerous‿surface
concise‿statement*	chief‿financial officer	relief‿from
giraffe*‿footprint	enough‿fanfare	perceive*‿vengeance
receive‿vitamins*	attractive*‿vocalist	comparative*‿volumes

English␣sheepdog	establish␣shelter	Irish␣shamrock
lavish␣chateau	finish␣shipment	brush␣sheepskin
crush␣sheetrock	splash␣shampoo	both␣things
worth␣thirty	fourth␣Thursday	underneath␣thistle

NOTE: A final "e" is silent in the words identified with an asterisk*.

Sentences

1. *The salesperson inquired about the bridesmaid's dress␣size.*
2. *The nurse␣supervisor complained about the continuous␣siren of the ambulance.*
3. *The chief␣financial officer reported that their assets were worth␣thirty million dollars.*
4. *The attractive␣vocalist performed in a lavish␣chateau for a charity fundraiser.*
5. *The waitress␣served us dinner and informed us that they have a guest chef on the fourth␣Thursday of each month.*
6. The bus␣sign said there was express␣service and local service available at that stop.
7. Be careful not to splash␣shampoo on the bathroom floor.
8. The hikers had to establish␣shelter during the ice␣storm.
9. On St. Patrick's Day, they decorated the walls with Irish␣shamrocks.
10. I bought both␣things at the enormous␣sale on July fourth.

15. Voiced Fricatives (/z/, /v/, "th" or /ð/) + Other Consonants

CD
2:29

Remember to link the final sound with the beginning of the next word.

is␣beneficial	was␣finished	has␣completed
choose␣books*	approve*␣purchases	pave*␣roads
achieve␣success*	give*␣presents	breathe*␣deeply
teethe␣painfully*	bathe*␣frequently	clothe*␣lavishly

NOTE: A final "e" is silent in the words identified with an asterisk*.

Sentences

1. Jake will appro**ve** purchases before they are ordered.
2. Karen wa**s** finished with the book by the end of the trip.
3. The doctor said, "Brea**the** deeply."
4. Sheryl will choo**se** books for the book club each month.
5. Roberta likes to ba**the** frequently in her whirlpool bathtub.
6. The children love to gi**ve** presents as much as receive them.
7. The county will pa**ve** roads after the winter.
8. Mike ha**s** completed his driver's education class.

16. Affricates ("ch" or /tʃ/ and "j" or /dʒ/) + Vowels

Remember to link the final sound with the beginning of the next word.

each other	teach us	pitch in
watch out	sketch artist	batch of…
catch a …	language* acquisition	patch up
poach eggs	switch into	cottage* industry
dosage amount*	botch up	wage* earner
backstage entrance*	pledge* amount	sausage* and eggs

NOTE: A final "e" is silent in the words identified with an asterisk*.

Sentences

1. *Mit**ch** and Midge looked at ea**ch** other and decided to poa**ch** eggs for breakfast.*
2. *There is a talented sket**ch** artist who works at the bea**ch** every weekend.*
3. *Gena needed to pat**ch** up the leaks in his roof.*
4. *Can you tea**ch** us how to dance the cha-cha?*
5. *Janie made a bat**ch** of her delicious chocolate brownies for the auction.*
6. If you could pit**ch** in and help with these dishes, that would be great.
7. The doctor indicated the dosa**ge** amount on his prescription pad.

> 8. The actors snuck into the theatre by the backstage⌣entrance to avoid the photographers.
>
> 9. The speech⌣and language pathologist knew about childhood language⌣acquisition.
>
> 10. Creating handmade jewelry can be a lucrative cottage⌣industry.

17. Affricates ("ch" or /tʃ/ and "j" or /dʒ/) + Consonants

> *Remember to link the final sound with the beginning of the next word.*
>
> | | | |
> |---|---|---|
> | *such⌣poverty* | search⌣party | badge⌣number |
> | *arch⌣support* | catch⌣phrase | fudge⌣sauce |
> | *clutch⌣purse* | match⌣maker | much⌣money |

Sentences

> 1. *The Peace Corps volunteer said that she had never seen such⌣poverty.*
> 2. *The police called off the search⌣party after the body was found.*
> 3. *What badge⌣number was he wearing?*
> 4. *I need to buy shoes with a good arch⌣support.*
> 5. *Would you like fudge⌣sauce on your ice cream sundae?*
> 6. The actress held a beaded clutch⌣purse as she strolled down the red carpet.
> 7. In some countries, a girl might rely on a match⌣maker to find a suitable husband.
> 8. Nikki made so much⌣money when she worked over her winter break.

18. Final /z/ + Consonant

> *Remember to link the final sound with the beginning of the next word.*
>
> | | | |
> |---|---|---|
> | *administers⌣medication* | sings⌣loudly | phones⌣customers |
> | *plans⌣projects* | begs⌣relentlessly | jogs⌣faithfully |
> | *kneels⌣reverently* | fails⌣miserably | assumes⌣responsibility |
> | *screens⌣candidates* | climbs⌣mountains | frames⌣pictures |

Sentences

1. Charles administers‿*m*edications to the residents after each meal.
2. Jayden sing*s‿l*oudly in music class.
3. Russell phone*s‿c*ustomers from hi*s‿c*ar on hi*s‿w*ay to the office.
4. Anne plan*s‿p*rojects for the upcoming theatre season.
5. Kathleen'*s‿d*og beg*s‿r*elentlessly when there i*s‿f*ood on the table.
6. Rita jog*s‿f*aithfully around Central Park every morning.
7. Nate fail*s‿m*iserably when he strives for perfection all of the time.
8. The manager assume*s‿r*esponsibility for the breakdown in communication.
9. The Human Resources manager screen*s‿c*andidates by reviewing their résumés.
10. Marjorie frame*s‿p*ictures of her children and display*s‿th*em proudly.

19. Final /dz/ and /zd/ + Consonant

CD 3:1

Remember to link the final sound with the beginning of the next word.

finds‿refuge	feeds‿hungry	loads‿packages
rides‿motorcycles	leads‿discussions	spreads‿news
needs‿volunteers	reads‿memos	grades‿papers
raised‿cattle	posed‿cooperatively	revised‿policies

Sentences

1. Sarah is a project manager who lea**ds‿d**iscussions and invites questions.
2. The food bank serves the community and fee**ds‿h**ungry children.
3. That stock boy cheerfully loa**ds‿p**ackages into customers' cars.
4. Carlos ri**des‿m**otorcycles as a hobby.
5. The animal shelter nee**ds‿v**olunteers to care for abandoned kittens and puppies.
6. Janie rea**ds‿m**emos and e-mails before starting her workday.
7. Jeremy sprea**ds‿** news to the entire family about his promotion.
8. The farmer rai**sed‿c**attle in the mountainous region of the state.

9. The model po**sed** cooperatively during the long photo-shoot.

10. The new administration revi**sed** polices from the previous legislature.

20. Final /v/ + Consonants

> Remember to link the final sound with the beginning of the next word.
>
> | | | |
> |---|---|---|
> | approve* purchases | pave* roads | crave* rewards |
> | give* directions | achieve* notoriety | weave* carelessly |
> | wave* goodbye | drive* slowly | leave* suddenly |
>
> NOTE: A final "e" is silent in the words identified with an asterisk*.

Sentences:

1. Jordan tries not to wea**ve** carelessly through traffic when he is tired.
2. The supervisor must appro**ve** purchases before they are ordered.
3. Please stop and gi**ve** directions before you proceed any further.
4. The politician will achie**ve** notoriety from his quick response in the crisis.
5. We must take a detour while they pa**ve** roads this summer.
6. Don't forget to wa**ve** goodbye as we drive away.
7. Why did Mariel lea**ve** suddenly when Ali entered the room?
8. Dri**ve** slowly when the roads are slick.

©2006, RULES

14. /t/ Variations

CD
3:3

You can pronounce the /t/ sound different ways depending on its position in the word or the sentence. The following rules identify different /t/ variations:

P - It is said "crisply" or "precisely," if it is in the beginning of a word or in the stressed syllable of a word; for example, "*T*om," "a*t*omic," "a*tt*ack."

F - Before an unstressed syllable, it is said more quickly, less precisely, and with some voicing as a flap /t/; for example, "a*tt*ic," "ci*t*y."

U - At the end of a word, it is unreleased and hardly heard; for example, "a*t*."

G - /t/ in the middle of a word that ends with an /n/ is sometimes said towards the back of the throat or as a glottal /t/; for example, "sa*t*in" ("sah- in").

C - When combined with other consonants in a cluster, the /t/ assumes the characteristics of the sounds in that blend; for example, "corre*ct*," "acce*pt*," "fir*st*," "le*ft*," "re*nt*," "pa*rt*," "be*lt*."

NOTE: When you link a word that has an unreleased /t/ ("put") with a word beginning with a vowel ("it"), the unreleased /t/ becomes a flap /t/; for example, "put‿it‿in," "a lot‿of," "meet‿us later." Linking is identified by "‿".
For additional information see Unit 13 - Linking Words Together.

Precise /t/

CD
3:4

The /t/ is pronounced "crisply" when it appears in the beginning of a word or in the stressed syllable of a word.

Say the following words with a Precise /t/:

*t*echnology	a*tt*ire	exper*t*ise
*t*orture	volun*t*eer	*t*eacher
*t*ailor	*t*enuous	a*t*omic
a*tt*endance	*t*ogether	*t*oothpaste
*t*omorrow	pho*t*ographer	au*t*onomy
*t*oo	*t*angible	*t*orrential
*t*own	*t*urn	*t*imid

<u>t</u>ired	<u>t</u>ennis	<u>t</u>ears
<u>t</u>able	<u>t</u>elephone	anti<u>c</u>ipate
<u>t</u>eenagers	<u>T</u>uesday	<u>t</u>epid
<u>t</u>errible	<u>t</u>ournament	<u>t</u>errain
<u>t</u>apestry	<u>t</u>earful	<u>t</u>elemetry
<u>t</u>ower	<u>t</u>ough	<u>t</u>urnover

Sentences

1. <u>T</u>om's exper<u>t</u>ise was in the <u>t</u>echnology field.
2. The <u>t</u>eacher requested a volun<u>t</u>eer to help <u>t</u>ake the <u>t</u>en <u>t</u>eenagers on a picnic.
3. The <u>t</u>ailor designed fashionable a<u>tt</u>ire.
4. The <u>t</u>orrential rain flooded the <u>t</u>emple down the road.
5. The <u>t</u>elephone is on the <u>t</u>able near the <u>t</u>oy closet.
6. After losing the <u>t</u>ennis match, <u>T</u>ara's eyes were filled with <u>t</u>ears.
7. <u>T</u>ogether, we made <u>t</u>enuous plans to a<u>tt</u>end the graduation.
8. The <u>t</u>avern is on the same side of the road as the <u>t</u>own hall.
9. <u>T</u>ammy is <u>t</u>imid when she is <u>t</u>ired.
10. A<u>tt</u>endance was good on <u>T</u>uesday, but poor on Sunday.
11. <u>T</u>erry was looking for <u>t</u>angible rewards.
12. Is your <u>t</u>urn <u>t</u>oday or <u>t</u>omorrow?
13. <u>T</u>ony swims with an inner <u>t</u>ube on the <u>t</u>epid river.
14. <u>T</u>ake your <u>t</u>ime and finish the <u>t</u>est.
15. <u>T</u>im bought a new <u>t</u>oothbrush and a <u>t</u>ube of <u>t</u>oothpaste.

Flap /t/

Before an unstressed syllable, /t/ is said more quickly, less precisely, and with slight voicing as in "a<u>tt</u>ic." It almost sounds like a /d/ sound.

CD
3:5

Repeat the following words and sentences using a Flap /t/:

ska<u>t</u>ing	limi<u>t</u>ed	productivi<u>t</u>y
abili<u>t</u>y	no<u>t</u>ify	capi<u>t</u>al
ci<u>t</u>izen	hospi<u>t</u>al	integri<u>t</u>y

sweater	visitor	waiting
motor	promoted	quality
water	flutter	velocity
automatic	society	density
mortar	diluted	security
recital	fitting	identity
better	epitome	matter

Sentences

1. *The visitor is waiting for the meeting to begin.*
2. *There are limited skating hours on the weekend.*
3. *He is responsible for security in the hospital.*
4. *Russ thinks it's better to grind spices with a mortar and pestle.*
5. *Without adequate capital, productivity may be compromised.*
6. The school is promoting high quality education.
7. Our automatic dishwasher needs a new motor.
8. Please notify me when the visitor arrives.
9. She has been promoted to president of the Honor Society.
10. The sparrow was fluttering around the water in the bird bath.
11. We have limited ability to influence the decision makers.
12. Does it matter that she is not a citizen?
13. They were waiting for the ballet recital to begin.
14. Our society reveres Hollywood celebrities.
15. Drink a lot of water after the competitive ice skating championship.

Unreleased /t/

> When /t/ occurs at the end of a word, it is considered unreleased and is barely heard. In sentences, when an unreleased /t/ is followed by a word with a vowel, the /t/ is linked and produced as a flap /t/; for example, "a lot‿ of money."

Repeat the following words, practicing an Unreleased /t/:

shirt	thought	got
bet	incorporate	private
benefit	wait	about
caught	doubt	fought
great	chart	alert
expert	yet	complete
debate	circuit	alright
highlight	walnut	peanut
chestnut	hazelnut	heat
bought	fight	night

Sentences

1. She got ‿a great shirt ‿at the sale.
2. Jim was a great speaker on the debate team.
3. Would you like to have hazelnut‿or chestnut-flavored coffee?
4. I doubt that the art benefit will raise much money for the organization.
5. The expert will complete his presentation before the morning is over.
6. What‿is the problem with the circuit breaker?
7. Wait; I thought you were not going.
8. Alright; I will get the information tonight.
9. What ‿is it ‿about the chart that you do not ‿understand?
10. We have to complete the report ‿and send it ‿in.
11. The highlight ‿of the night was the private party.
12. He felt ‿it was only right to fight for his country.
13. Kit put her coat ‿on the seat.
14. I met them on a hot summer night.
15. Please wait to get ‿on the boat.

©2006, RULES

Glottal /t/

CD
3:7

> /t/ in the middle of a word that ends with an /n/ is sometimes said towards the back of the throat as a glottal /t/ as in "satin" ("sah-in"). You should feel a "catch" between your vocal cords as if you are saying "uh-oh."

Say the following words with a "catch" in the throat for the Glottal /t/:

button	cotton	kitten
written	bitten	smitten
rotten	tighten	whiten
frightening	heighten	forgotten
certain	maintenance	mountain
important	remittance	shorten
monotonous	brighten	threaten

Sentences

1. What kind of button would you like on your cotton sweater?
2. The satin wedding gown is gorgeous.
3. Don't frighten the kitten by pulling its tail.
4. I'm certain that he's forgotten that we were in the same school.
5. We have to heighten our awareness of cultural differences.
6. How can I whiten my teeth before the reunion next month?
7. I have to tighten my oral appliance.
8. His voice was monotonous during the lecture.
9. I found one mitten, but I'm missing the other.
10. Was she bitten by a wild animal?
11. She is smitten with her dance teacher.
12. It is important to have the right equipment when you hike up the mountain.
13. Are you certain that the apple is rotten?
14. Where is the remittance for the maintenance work?
15. He had written a threatening message.

Cluster /t/

When combined with other consonants, the /t/ assumes the characteristics of the sounds in that cluster and is often more prominent and released, e.g., "correct," "accept," "first," "left," or, depending on regional dialects, it may be unreleased, e.g., "rent," "part," and "belt."

Clusters may be found in the initial, medial, and final position of words. They are also called consonant blends.

As these words are linked in sentences, sometimes the cluster is reduced or altered; for example, "won-chu," "firs- time."

Say the following words aloud, being sure to pronounce all of the sounds in the Consonant Cluster:

co**st**	ju**st**	fir**st**
la**st**	wo**n't**	do**n't**
ca**n't**	should**n't**	aspe**ct**
co**sts**	stateme**nts**	te**sts**
mome**nt**	quotie**nt**	apartme**nt**
denti**st**	ca**st**	so**ft**
bla**st**	mu**st**	torme**nt**
le**ft**	resi**st**	restri**ct**
resista**nt**	confli**ct**	acce**pt**
suspe**ct**	inspe**ct**	scri**pt**
infli**ct**	a**pt**	ade**pt**
difficu**lt**	be**lt**	fau**lt**

Sentences

1. Fir**st** ‿a minstrel performed and then an art**ist** showed us how to make stained glass.
2. The apartme**nt** ‿ is tremendous and it is on the le**ft** side of the street.
3. Resi**st** the temptation to acce**pt** the fir**st** ‿amou**nt** ‿on the li**st**.
4. It was difficu**lt** to control the ca**sts'** ‿outbur**sts** during rehearsal.
5. The criminal mu**st** stand trial because the ballisti**cs** te**sts** ‿implicated him.
6. They will have to redire**ct** ‿or dive**rt** traffic as the runners pass the monume**nt**.

7. The university has a restri<u>ct</u>ed admissions policy for immigra<u>nts</u>.

8. Shelley was resista<u>nt</u> to those antibiotics after the la<u>st</u> bout of pneumonia.

9. The magnet mu<u>st</u> be te<u>st</u>ed for particle contamination.

10. Do<u>n't</u> trim that che<u>st</u>nut tree without checking for mi<u>tes</u>!

11. Can you corre<u>ct</u> the quotie<u>nt</u> in this difficu<u>lt</u> equation?

12. The e<u>xt</u>erminator inspe<u>ct</u>ed the house for inse<u>cts</u> and rode<u>nts</u>.

Combinations of /t/

The following words and sentences have a combination of /t/ variations within the same word. Pronounce the words correctly, using Precise, Unreleased, Glottal, Flap, and/or Cluster variations as indicated. Some of the words may have multiple pronunciations depending on regional dialects. **NOTE:** Write the letter above the /t/ to identify the /t/ variation and help pronunciation. The first one is done for you.

P U		
<u>t</u>arge<u>t</u>	ten<u>t</u>a<u>t</u>ive	<u>t</u>en<u>ts</u>
a<u>tt</u>itude	al<u>t</u>i<u>t</u>ude	ac<u>t</u>ive
ac<u>t</u>ivi<u>t</u>y	ar<u>t</u>icula<u>t</u>e	ar<u>t</u>icle
<u>T</u>oron<u>t</u>o	in<u>t</u>eres<u>t</u>	scien<u>t</u>is<u>ts</u>
pho<u>t</u>ographic	pho<u>t</u>ography	<u>t</u>eapo<u>t</u>
for<u>t</u>y	four<u>t</u>een	seven<u>t</u>y-eigh<u>t</u>
<u>t</u>o<u>ts</u>	an<u>t</u>icipa<u>t</u>e	con<u>t</u>es<u>t</u>
scrip<u>ts</u>	ornamen<u>t</u>	<u>t</u>ournamen<u>t</u>
in<u>t</u>ermedia<u>t</u>e	res<u>t</u>auran<u>t</u>	con<u>t</u>inen<u>t</u>al
<u>t</u>elecomp<u>t</u>er	presen<u>t</u>ation	consul<u>t</u>an<u>t</u>

Sentences
1. The <u>t</u>wo friends pitched their <u>t</u>en<u>ts</u> a<u>t</u> a high al<u>t</u>i<u>t</u>ude.

2. The <u>t</u>ouris<u>ts</u> flocked <u>t</u>o the moun<u>t</u>ain retrea<u>t</u> for relaxation and renewal.

3. <u>T</u>oron<u>t</u>o is an in<u>t</u>eres<u>t</u>ing place to explore.

4. The scien<u>t</u>is<u>ts</u> an<u>t</u>icipa<u>t</u>ed a trea<u>t</u>men<u>t</u> would be discovered for this frigh<u>t</u>ening disease.

5. The ar<u>t</u>is<u>t</u>ic professor repor<u>t</u>ed the reviews of a new exhibi<u>t</u>.

6. <u>T</u>erry purchased a <u>t</u>eapo<u>t</u> a<u>t</u> <u>T</u>arge<u>t</u> for <u>t</u>wen<u>t</u>y dollars.

7. There were only four<u>t</u>een res<u>t</u>ric<u>t</u>ed-view <u>t</u>icke<u>ts</u> remaining.

8. I have tentative plans to contact my old roommate when I am on vacation in Toledo.

9. The tots were treated for smoke inhalation.

10. The bacteria were resistant to antibiotics.

11. Shall we institute a new termination policy?

12. Betty has a good attitude about her new job responsibilities.

13. Todd's transcripts will be in the Bursar's Office in September.

14. Is this photography course considered beginner or intermediate level?

15. The restaurant will be closed beginning tomorrow while they exterminate and renovate.

Exercise 3: Take the /t/ Challenge

Read the sentences aloud. First, focus on one type of /t/ variation and then build on that until you can focus on all of them. Remember, there may be more than one way to say the /t/. Good luck!

Precise /t/ + Unreleased /t/ Sentences:

1. How can technology benefit our great society?
2. My great aunt has expertise in photography and teaching tennis to teens.
3. I'm going to town tomorrow to buy a terrific new shirt.
4. I told my doctor that I think I am allergic to peanut sauce.
5. The volunteer will be back here on Tuesday to help with the silent auction.
6. Tom will use the telephone to solicit private donations.
7. In the heat of the night, things can turn ugly.
8. I thought we would have a tearful goodbye and I was right.
9. Please alert me if there is a problem with this terrible circuit breaker.
10. Kit took a turn for the worse in the middle of the night.

Precise /t/ + Unreleased /t/ + Cluster /t/ Sentences

1. How many tests on statistics can they torture me with at college?
2. Your apartment is not on a fault line or near the electrical tower, is it?
3. Will you wait in the car for me for a moment while I drop this x-ray at my dentist's office?

4. The Medieval tapestry scholar talked about how difficult it was to weave during the turbulent Middle Ages.
5. I doubt she is adept at chess tournaments.
6. The teacher told his students that the virus is resistant to the latest medical advancements.
7. I just don't want to eat a walnut right now.
8. What will it cost to inspect the old barn in town?

Precise /t/ + Unreleased /t/ + Cluster /t/ + Glottal /t/ Sentences

1. Bleach will brighten that old cotton shirt that the tailor made for you in Toronto.
2. Tina had forgotten to tell you how the terrible teacher liked to inflict pain on the innocent children at the orphanage.
3. I'll be certain to read the script and make cast suggestions by this time tomorrow.
4. Tuan was bitten by a timid kitten and must take medicine for ten days and nights.
5. Tori inquired if this belt restricts your movement when you tighten it on the last notch.
6. She wrote an important note along with her remittance payment to the telephone company.

Precise /t/ + Unreleased /t/ + Cluster /t/ + Glottal /t/ + Flap /t/ Sentences

1. It is better to select a sweater when you go skating than to wear a cotton shirt like when you play tennis or racquetball.
2. Please tell the hospital security person when a visitor attempts to enter a restricted area that might threaten classified documents.
3. Water quality is important and must be inspected by sophisticated tests by people who know about the water treatment system in their town or community.

4. We thought it would be better to take a bicycle tour of the mountainous Italian countryside rather than to try to bicycle in the cities crowded with international tourists.

15. Other /t/ Pronunciations

CD 3:9

> **1.** When a /t/ is joined with **-ion** as a suffix, the pronunciation becomes "sh" or [ʃ] and is pronounced like "**shun**" or [ʃən].
>
> educa**tion**   saluta**tion**   vaca**tion**   dicta**tion**

*Say the following words and sentences and pronounce the "-**tion**" correctly:*

elec**tion**	dona**tion**	extradi**tion**	carna**tion**
cau**tion**	publica**tion**	devo**tion**	po**tion**
immigra**tion**	ova**tion**	specializa**tion**	ra**tion**
emo**tion**	lo**tion**	mo**tion**	informa**tion**
dic**tion**	men**tion**	edi**tion**	communica**tion**
termina**tion**	collabora**tion**	investiga**tion**	transporta**tion**
amputa**tion**	adop**tion**	frac**tion**	tradi**tion**
gradua**tion**	frustra**tion**	applica**tion**	rota**tion**
inten**tion**	dehydra**tion**	prosecu**tion**	nota**tion**
demonstra**tion**	evolu**tion**	punctua**tion**	pronuncia**tion**

Sentences - First underline the **-ion** suffix and then read the sentences aloud.

1. The aromatic lotion had a faint lavender scent.
2. There was an ongoing federal investigation into the transportation accident.
3. After the election, the politician promised to address issues of immigration and taxation.
4. The community college offered classes in mass communication and information technology.
5. "We'll have to ration our supplies," the troop leader announced with caution.
6. The military officer fought her extradition with determination.
7. Please don't mention my colleague's termination.
8. That publication is considered to be a final edition.
9. We were asked to make a donation or campaign contribution at the rally.
10. His specialization was in the design of motion detectors for security purposes.

> **2.** When a /t/ is joined with **-ial** as a suffix, the pronunciation becomes "sh" or [ʃ] and is pronounced like "shul" or [ʃəl].
>
> ini**tial**   confiden**tial**   deferen**tial**   torren**tial**

Say the following words and sentences and pronounce the "**-tial**" correctly:

residen**tial**	sequen**tial**	circumstan**tial**	differen**tial**
par**tial**	nup**tial**	mar**tial**	pala**tial**

Sentences – First underline the **-tial** suffix and then read the sentences aloud.

1. That residential part of town is known for its palatial homes.
2. Judo and karate are ancient martial arts.
3. I don't think he will be convicted on circumstantial evidence.
4. My initial reaction was deferential.
5. The customer made a partial payment, but still had outstanding debts to the credit card company.
6. Will they cancel the nuptials if there is torrential rain?
7. I told her to keep the news confidential.
8. The neuropsychologist made a differential diagnosis.
9. My grandparents discussed the influential people in their lives.
10. Please tell me how to assemble this device in sequential order.

> **3.** When a /t/ is joined with **-u**, the pronunciation often becomes "ch" or [ʧ].
>
> for**tu**ne   tor**tu**re   mor**tu**ary   si**tu**ation
>
> Exceptions: opportunity, fortuitous

Say the following words and sentences and pronounce the "**-tu**" correctly:

habi**tu**al	obi**tu**ary	perpe**tu**al	na**tu**ral
si**tu**ation	fac**tu**al	fluc**tu**ate	unfor**tu**nate

punctuation	virtual	amateur	capture
conjecture	culture	denture	fixture
furniture	moisture	future	lecture
mixture	picture	sculpture	structure
texture	manufacture	temperature	signature

Sentences – First underline the **-tu** and then read the sentences aloud.

1. *The lecture was on the topic of punctuation and grammar.*
2. *Where do they manufacture furniture in this state?*
3. *Is there a lot of moisture and high temperature in the estuary?*
4. *Lois is an amateur at sculpture design.*
5. *The designer is known for her mixture of color and texture.*
6. The photographer's pictures capture her subjects in natural settings.
7. The obituary was factual and unemotional.
8. Their household is in a perpetual state of confusion.
9. The light fixture needs to be repaired.
10. The temperature of the earth may continue to rise in the future.

16. Y- Insertion

1. When the vowel sound /u/ is spelled with the letter "u" or the letters "ew," a "Y" or /j/ sound is often heard in the pronunciation. Of course, there are many exceptions to this rule, which can be confusing to nonnative speakers of English.

CD
3:12

configuration *manufacture* *manual*

simulation *executive* *computer*

Remember that the vowel sound /u/ may be spelled as "ue" (blue), "u" (rule), "o" (movie), "oo" (soon), "ui" (fruit), "ou" (through), "ew" (few), "oe" (shoe), "eau" (beautiful), and "u + consonant + e" (tune).

Pronunciation With and Without Y-Insertions

Pronounce these words **with** a Y-insertion:

CD
3:12

molecule	*meticulous*	*mutation*	*miraculous*
communist	*university*	*futile*	*peculiar*
unity	*reputation*	*unanimous*	*fuel*

Pronounce these words **without** a Y-insertion:

conclude	*solution*	*rumor*	*nuclear*
rudimentary	*convoluted*	*resolution*	*lunatic*

Exercise 2: Indicate whether the underlined words should be pronounced as /u/ (OO) or /ju/ (Y) by writing the notation above the words. Write either "OO" for /u/ or "Y" for /ju/. Read the sentences aloud using the proper pronunciation for /u/.

1. <u>Stu's</u> <u>beautiful</u> fiancée <u>concluded</u> that she wanted <u>to</u> be married in <u>June</u> under a full <u>moon</u>.

2. Rodeo Drive is an <u>exclusive</u> shopping area in Los Angeles where <u>you</u> can find

unique shoes, clothing and jewels.

3. My new computer got good reviews in the consumer magazine.

4. The executive chef created a new spring menu using fresh local produce.

5. Susan thought that her math tutor was useless so she terminated her.

6. Lou always used his long commute as an excuse to be late for executive meetings.

7. We saw the musical even though it got bad reviews when it previewed on Broadway.

8. It is hard to chew food when you lose your teeth.

9. My nephew is a garrulous and humorous fellow.

10. June has a pug dog that has been described by her veterinarian as cute, enthusiastic, and easily confused.

11. The newspaper managing director screened résumés for a new food editor.

12. Do you use regular gasoline in your SUV?

13. My client knew numerous pronunciation rules and concluded that English was a peculiar language.

14. Let's continue our discussion of employment opportunities in the student union.

15. Parents are concerned that children who listen to music at loud volumes may have hearing problems in the future.

16. Few can argue that pollution is not a huge environmental issue.

17. The doctor assumed that the baby's immune system was still undeveloped at two weeks of age.

18. There was a huge accumulation of snow at high altitudes this winter.

19. If the pregnant woman doesn't go into labor by Tuesday, she will be induced.

20. The executive enthusiastically stated that communication is the most important work-related skill.

21. The humanitarian dedicated her life to serving impoverished communities.

22. The museum curator knew the value of paintings done during Picasso's blue period.

23. Andrew is a supervisor at a new distribution plant in Houston.

24. Prudence concluded that the faulty unit was still under warrantee.

25. Rudy strolled down the avenue, whistling happy tunes.

26. I assume that you would like Trudy to introduce you at the convention.

27. The university is now serving healthier food than it used to.

28. The soccer team does strenuous exercises so they can move quickly without injury.

29. May I please have a tissue to wipe this spill off my new suit?

30. Lucy received a few bruises on her shin after her loose shoelaces caused her to trip and fall.

17. -Y Ending Pronounced as /i/ "ee"

CD
3:13

*1. For nouns ending in a **consonant + y combination**, the -y is usually pronounced as a long /i/ sound. When making these nouns plural, change the -y to an "i" and add -es. Remember to pronounce the plural form with a long /i/ sound as well.*

baby / **babies**   **history** / **histories**   **city** / **cities**

Exercise 1: *Practice reading the following words and sentences aloud. Make sure that you pronounce the final -**y** as an /i/ sound.*

priority / priorities	directory / directories	memory / memories
boundary / boundaries	primary / primaries	phony / phonies
daisy / daisies	country / countries	company / companies

Sentences

1. *The career coach asked her client to list her job **priorities**.*
2. *The **baby** always cries when her mother leaves the room.*
3. *The nurse wrote down the patient's medical **history** on the intake form.*
4. *How many **cities** in Europe have you visited?*
5. *We need to replace our car **battery**.*
6. The mountain climber liked to push her physical and emotional **boundaries**.
7. The **primary** elections will be held in November.
8. Sasha picked a bouquet of **daisies** for her mother.
9. The employees were listed **alphabetically** in the company **directory**.
10. What are your favorite childhood **memories**?

CD
3:14

> *2. To change an adjective into an adverb, add **-ly** to adjectives ending in a single or double consonant cluster. Remember to pronounce the final **-y** as a long /i/ sound.*
>
> | | | |
> |---|---|---|
> | ***bold / boldly*** | ***formal / formally*** | ***deep / deeply*** |

Exercise 2: *Practice reading the following words and sentences aloud. Make sure that you pronounce the final -y as a long /i/ sound.*

friend / friendly	impetuous / impetuously	verbal / verbally
global / globally	superficial / superficially	patient / patiently
proud / proudly	peaceful / peacefully	perfect / perfectly
painful / painfully	splendid / splendidly	informal / informally
tearful / tearfully	joyful / joyfully	dismal / dismally

Sentences

1. *The victim **boldly** faced her accuser in the courtroom.*
2. *Evelyn waited **impatiently** for the bus to arrive.*
3. *She **proudly** accepted her honorary degree.*
4. *The storage bowls and lids fit **perfectly**.*
5. *After her swimming lesson, Jayden fell **soundly** asleep.*
6. He died **peacefully** in his sleep.
7. John's Scottish band performed **splendidly** at the competition.
8. Russ **painfully** wrapped an ace bandage around his injured knee.
9. Lydia entertained her guests **informally**.
10. Marty answered the questions **briefly**.

3. *For adjectives ending in **-cal**, when the **-ly** is added to make it an adverb, a syllable is reduced and it is pronounced as "klee," e.g. automatically → "automatik-klee."*

basic / basically   **typical / typically**   **practical / practically**

Exercise 3: *Practice reading the following words and sentences aloud. Make sure that you pronounce the final **-y** as a long /i/ sound.*

alphabetical / alphabetically	chronological / chronologically
magical / magically	historical / historically
logical / logically	identical / identically
political / politically	statistical / statistically
typical / typically	mathematical / mathematically
chemical / chemically	technical / technically

Sentences

1. *Kang explained the information very **technically**.*
2. *The two young girls were dressed **identically**.*
3. *Jiamin conducted the research **systematically**.*
4. *We **typically** meet in the conference room.*
5. ***Historically**, the natives were able to hunt for their own food.*
6. They were **politically** active as students at the University of Maryland.
7. The woman **magically** appeared in the locked box.
8. Ben was **mathematically** inclined and performed well on all exams.
9. Can you report the events **chronologically**?
10. We were **practically** finished by the time Hexin arrived.

4. *For adjectives ending in -e, add -ly to make it an adverb and pronounce the -y as a long /i/.*

polite/politely   **nice/nicely**   **time/timely**

CD
3:16

Exercise 4: Practice reading the following words and sentences aloud. Make sure that you pronounce the -ly ending as a long /i/ sound.

time / timely	*late / lately*	*shape / shapely*
complete / completely	*precise / precisely*	*separate / separately*
considerate / considerately	*desperate / desperately*	*fortunate / fortunately*

Sentences

1. Melanie finished her project in a **timely** manner.
2. Philip has been feeling much better **lately**.
3. Shelley filled out the application **precisely**.
4. Kim **desperately** needed to get away on a vacation.
5. They identified the thief **separately**.
6. **Fortunately**, she avoided a traffic accident.
7. After lifting weights for six weeks, her muscles were **shapely**.
8. Nikki is **completely** packed for her vacation.
9. Joanne **considerately** prepared dinner for Phil.
10. Martin **accurately** completed the documents.

5. *For adjectives ending in -ble, drop the -e and add -ly in order to make it into an adverb. Remember to reduce the -ble syllable and pronounce the -ly as a long /i/; for example, incredible → "incredibl‿ee," not "incredibul-lee."*

possible / possibly   **visible / visibly**   **nimble / nimbly**

CD
3:17

©2006, RULES

Exercise 5: *Practice reading the following words and sentences aloud. Make sure that you pronounce the -ly ending as a long /i/ sound.*

amicable / amicably	agreeable / agreeably	audible / audibly
honorable / honorably	comfortable / comfortably	terrible / terribly
probable / probably	preferable / preferably	incredible / incredibly
remarkable / remarkably	unbelievable / unbelievably	credible / credibly
sensible / sensibly	respectable / respectably	legible / legibly

Sentences

1. *It will **probably** be the rainiest June on record.*
2. *Roberta's van can seat eight people **comfortably**.*
3. ***Incredibly**, the high school play was sold-out in one day.*
4. *We will miss you **terribly** when you live overseas for a year.*
5. *Please write your name **legibly** on this form.*
6. The nutritionist told her patient to eat **sensibly** if she wanted to maintain her weight.
7. The cat **nimbly** climbed the tree.
8. The host **agreeably** showed everyone the way.
9. Lorraine looked **remarkably** good for her age.
10. The friends treated each other **amicably**.

Exercise 6: Practice reading the following words and sentences aloud. Make sure that you pronounce the -**ly** ending as a long /i/ sound.

6. The following miscellaneous words end in -**y** and are pronounced with a final /i/ sound.

pity	penalty	penny	pathology
policy	poverty	pottery	pony
pulley	prickly	sickly	perjury
personality	publicity	supposedly	versatility
portability	privacy	piracy	bankruptcy
slippery	preparatory	apathy	monopoly

secondary	blueberry	compatibility	bossy
calamity	strawberry	sanitary	inflammatory

Sentences

1. It will be a **pity** if we have to postpone the **party** due to rain.
2. The corporate executive was convicted on five counts of **perjury** and obstruction of justice.
3. Isabel has a cheerful **personality**.
4. Do you know how to play the game **Monopoly**™?
5. I think that **company** just declared **bankruptcy**.
6. The students are taking a **preparatory** course prior to their board exams.
7. The patient described her chief complaint and **secondary** symptoms.
8. It was a **calamity** when the basement flooded for a third time.
9. Be careful walking on the pool deck as it can get very **slippery**.
10. Please don't act **bossy** if you want me to do something for you!

Exercise 7: Practice reading the following sentences aloud. Make sure that you pronounce the final **-y** as a long /i/ sound.

7. The following miscellaneous words end in **-e** and are pronounced as an /i/ sound.

recipe	catastrophe	hyperbole	apostrophe
epitome	committee	employee	lessee

Sentences

1. What is your favorite **recipe** for Thanksgiving dinner?
2. Please remember to put an **apostrophe** after the "-s."
3. Hurricane Katrina was a terrible **catastrophe**.
4. Winning the Oscar award was the **epitome** of her acting career.
5. They learned how to identify a **hyperbole** in their English class.
6. The **committee** met once a week.
7. Victor was selected as the **employee** of the month.
8. The contract was signed between the lessor and the **lessee**.

18. Syllable Reductions

**CD
3:18**

> **1.** *In English, many words with three or more syllables are "reduced" by eliminating the syllable with the weakest stress so that the word flows more smoothly and naturally. The pronunciation may vary from region to region, but the following are some typical examples. The letters in parentheses are not always pronounced.*
>
> | | | |
> |---|---|---|
> | *veg(e)table* | *basic(a)lly* | *comf(or)table* |
> | *lab(o)ratory* | *bus(i)ness* | *ev(e)ry* |
> | *We(d)n(e)sday* | *fav(o)rite* | *temp(e)rature* |

Exercise 1: Look at the following words and <u>circle</u> the syllable that is reduced. Then say the words with the reduced syllable and say these words in sentences.

aspirin	automatically	average
beverage	broccoli	business
camera	Catholic	chocolate
comfortable	comparable	conference
deliberate	delivery	respiratory
diamond	difference	different
drapery	elaborate (adjective)	evening
every	factory	favorite
general	history	interest
interesting	jewelry	laboratory
liberal	listening	mystery
nauseous	corporate	omelet
practically	reference	restaurant
several	separate (adjective)	temperature
temporary	vegetable	victory
Wednesday	convenient	salient

2. *When a "c" is followed by the suffix* **-ial** *or* **-ian***, the suffix is pronounced as "sh" or [ʃ] and sounds like [ʃəl] or [ʃən].*

spe**cial**	finan**cial**	benefi**cial**
offi**cial**	so**cial**	beauti**cian**
clini**cian**	pediatri**cian**	opti**cian**

Exercise 2: Mark the syllables that can be reduced and then say the sentences aloud. The first one is done for you.

1. She received diamond jewelry for her twentieth anniversary.
2. On Wednesday, Larry went to the Farmers' Market to buy fresh vegetables.
3. Philip had elevated temperature due to his respiratory infection.
4. Joanne attended a conference for the Catholic Charities.
5. While traveling in business class, Martin received unlimited alcoholic beverages.
6. After the elaborate introduction, the audience was listening carefully.
7. Nicole felt nauseous after she took the aspirin on an empty stomach.
8. Each and every reference must be cited carefully in the report.
9. Michael's new camera automatically focuses on the subject.
10. David deliberately avoided his favorite restaurant on his special birthday.
11. The break-in at the laboratory remained a mystery to practically all of the investigators.
12. The two comfortable meeting rooms were comparable in costs but different in convenience.
13. The chef prepared quite an interesting omelet!
14. The demonstration brought several million people to Washington, DC.
15. That factory manufactured exquisite drapery.
16. In general, I try to avoid chocolate whenever possible.
17. The delivery truck came four separate times until someone was there to receive the furniture.
18. They have a very liberal policy at the new nursery school.
19. The History teacher was just a temporary replacement for this semester.
20. His favorite vegetable was broccoli.

CD 3:20

3. *Reduction of Function Words*

Typically "function" words, such as conjunctions, prepositions, articles, as well as pronouns, are not stressed in conversational speech. We change them to make the important words, such as nouns, verbs, adjectives and adverbs, "stand out." When words are not stressed, they are said quickly and we often reduce the word. This is not necessary, but it improves the fluency of speaking American English. An example of this is with the word "and." Instead of pronouncing it clearly, it becomes 'n as in "room and board" → *"room 'n board."*

Exercise 3: *Say the following word pairs and concentrate on reducing the "and" to 'n.*

NOTE: Stress the second part of the word pair.

trial and error	shipping and handling	city and state
cut and paste	paper and pen	stop and go
sales and rentals	lock and key	mind and body
boys and girls	ladies and gentlemen	health and fitness
arts and entertainment	song and dance	wait and see
rock and roll	parks and recreation	wash and dry
business and finance	sales and marketing	cast and crew
front and center	fun and games	in and out
on and off	coffee and tea	cake and ice cream
shoes and socks	surf and turf	bread and butter
vitamins and minerals	hamburger and fries	beans and rice
peanut butter and jelly	beer and wine	cheese and crackers
soup and salad	track and field	peas and carrots
R and D (research and development)		I and O (input and output)

Exercise 4: Underline "and" in the following sentences. When you read them aloud, reduce "and" to 'n where appropriate.

1. My favorite newspaper sections are <u>Health and Fitness</u> and <u>Arts and Entertainment</u>.

2. The diner serves hamburgers and fries along with cake and ice cream.

3. Excuse me, but could we please have some bread and butter with our soup and salad?

4. The cast and crew celebrated their award with beer and wine.

5. You can purchase vitamins and minerals in the "Mind and Body" section of the health food store.

6. The boys and girls played Hide and Seek in the playground.

7. I have a magazine subscription to both <u>Travel and Leisure</u> and <u>Food and Wine</u>.

8. The Parks and Recreation Department is repairing the town's track and field for the summer.

9. The host said, "Ladies and Gentlemen; please help yourselves to cheese and crackers until our guest speaker arrives."

10. There was stop and go traffic during rush hour.

11. It may seem otherwise, but sales and marketing is not always fun and games.

12. I need to buy some new shoes and socks.

13. I want to go out to dinner for some surf and turf.

14. I don't know why, but my internet connection keeps going on and off.

15. My daughter likes to eat peanut butter and jelly sandwiches for lunch.

16. My cat keeps going in and out of our yard.

17. The ballet teacher told the children to line up front and center for the recital.

18. Aren't you too old to listen to rock and roll music?

19. My cousin is an expert in the field of business and finance.

20. You can buy coffee and tea in bulk at the food store.

19. Past Tense Endings

CD
3:21

> 1. **Final _voiceless_ sounds**, (/k/, /p/, /f/, "sh" or /ʃ/, "ch" or /ʧ/, and /s/), add a /t/ sound when pronouncing the regular past tense -**ed** ending.
>
> **walked (t)**　　**stopped (t)**　　**washed (t)**　　**coughed (t)**

Exercise 1: Practice reading the following words and sentences aloud. Make sure that you pronounce the -ed as a /t/ when the last sound heard in the root word is voiceless. Remember to link the words together in the sentences.

brushed	asked	whipped	talked
licked	stopped	researched	looked
cherished	provoked	sacrificed	balanced
linked	increased	conversed	reimbursed
checked	published	rehearsed	introduced
videotaped	approached	accomplished	processed
experienced	marched	laughed	wished

Sentences

1. She brush**ed**‿aside her fears and approach**ed**‿the podium.
2. The baby lick**ed**‿the whipp**ed**‿cream off the cake.
3. The accountant check**ed**‿the expense records and then reimburs**ed** ‿the employee.
4. The students research**ed**‿all of the available publish**ed**‿works on their chosen topic.
5. The bank link**ed**‿ her checking and savings accounts.
6. We stopp**ed**‿and introduc**ed**‿ourselves to our new neighbors.
7. We convers**ed**‿about many interesting topics.
8. We look**ed**‿at the beautiful paintings and then talk**ed**‿about how they made us feel.
9. She ask**ed**‿her grandmother for her cherish**ed**‿ locket.

10. We rehears**ed**‿our presentation and then videotap**ed**‿ourselves.

11. They increas**ed**‿the training budget for next year.

12. Are the programs balanc**ed**‿and fair?

13. They ask**ed**‿the employees to sign non-compete agreements.

14. She was focus**ed**‿and successfully accomplish**ed**‿her goals.

15. He was experienc**ed**‿in dealing with international legal processes.

---

2. *Final <u>voiced</u> sounds*, (/g/, /b/, /v/, "j" or /dʒ/, "th" or /ð/, /z/, /l/, /m/, /n/, and /r/), and vowels add a /d/ sound when pronouncing the regular past tense -*ed* ending.

listened (d)	*showed (d)*	*loved (d)*	*bathed (d)*

CD 3:22

Exercise 2: *Practice reading the following words and sentences aloud. Make sure that you pronounce the "-ed" as a /d/ when the last sound heard in the root word is voiced. Remember to link the words together in the sentences.*

explained	bothered	reserved	prepared
manufactured	played	annoyed	smiled
ordered	refused	transformed	clarified
telephoned	explored	appeared	argued
justified	failed	admired	recognized
logged	robbed	raged	amazed
harmed	warned	called	tried

Sentences

1. *The Maitre'd explain**ed**‿that the vacant table was reserv**ed**‿for another customer.*

2. *The foreman was annoy**ed**‿that the manufacturer fail**ed**‿to deliver the parts on time.*

3. *The actress smil**ed**‿when she was recogniz**ed**‿by her fans.*

4. *I was bother**ed**‿when I receiv**ed**‿a parking ticket, even though the meter was broken.*

5. *My client telephon**ed**‿to cancel this morning's appointment.*

6. The recipe call**ed**‿for clarifi**ed**‿butter.

7. She felt transform**ed**‿ after a facial and a massage.

8. The secretary refus**ed**‿to put the call through to her boss.

9. We explor**ed**‿all of the options and agre**ed**‿upon a solution.

10. The response from management appear**ed**‿to be justifi**ed**.

©2006, RULES

11. The trial lawyers argu**ed** over the case.

12. She admir**ed** the dancer who play**ed** the leading role in the ballet.

13. Are you prepar**ed** for your interviews?

14. Were the devices manufactur**ed** in the United States?

15. I order**ed** a lot of items online this spring.

---

3. Final /t/ and /d/ consonants, add an extra *-ed [əd]* suffix. This suffix becomes a separate syllable.

want**ed** *(əd)*	need**ed** *(əd)*	content**ed** *(əd)*	exploit**ed** *(əd)*

Exercise 3: *Practice reading the following words and sentences aloud. Make sure that you pronounce the -ed as an -ed suffix [əd] when the last sound heard in the root word is either a /t/ or a /d/. Remember to link the words together in the sentences.*

appointed	appropriated	contested	converted
connected	adjusted	attended	responded
anticipated	demonstrated	added	marketed
regulated	commented	wasted	projected
invited	inspected	rejected	seated
started	regarded	irritated	protected

Sentences

1. *Who was appointed to lead the delegation?*

2. *Almost everyone in the organization attended the black-tie event.*

3. *The town set up a "swap-shop" so that unwanted items would not be wasted.*

4. *They responded by staging a protest.*

5. *The extensive renovations added value to the home.*

6. They market**ed** their services to professionals in the high-tech industry.

7. Geneticists are interest**ed** in up-regulat**ed** and down-regulat**ed** genes.

8. We anticipat**ed** a severe storm so we appropriat**ed** the necessary supplies.

9. The team members were remind**ed** to complete their surveys online.

10. Are these wires all connect**ed** properly?

11. The meteorologist comment**ed** on how much rain has accumulat**ed** this spring.

12. What are the project**ed** earnings for the next fiscal year?

13. The instructor demonstrat**ed** how the device should be insert**ed**.

14. Car insurance rates are adjust**ed** according to the driver's records.

15. Who stat**ed** that the will would be contest**ed**?

20. -S Endings

Plural nouns, possessive nouns, and third-person singular verbs all have -s endings. Most -s endings <u>DON'T</u> add an extra syllable. The only times an extra syllable is added is with words ending in /s/, /z/, "sh" or /ʃ/, "ch" or /tʃ/, "zh" or /ʒ/, and "j" or /dʒ/. The extra syllable is pronounced as "-ez" [əz].

CD
3:24

1. *Final voiceless consonants,* *(/p/, /t/, /k/, /f/, "th" or /θ/), add an /s/ sound, as follows:*

*tap**s***	*sit**s***	*talk**s***
*laugh**s***	*brief**s***	*moth**s***

Exercise 1: Practice reading the following words aloud. Make sure that you pronounce the **-s** ending as /s/ when the last sound heard in the root word is voiceless.

makes	lifts	sits
steps	cuts	sinks
crafts	writes	leaks
twists	locks	bumps
types	lists	trusts
pats	thinks	sheets
shuts	insights	recites
heats	whips	limits

Exercise 2: Underline the final **-s** in the following sentences and say them aloud. Remember to link the words together.

1. *Shannon makes beautiful arts and crafts projects.*
2. *The secretary types lists all day long.*
3. *The maid dislikes cleaning the sinks and changing the sheets.*
4. *Byrna pats her cat's head when she sits in the sunny window.*
5. *When Evelyn thinks about the accident, she shuts down.*

6. Carol trusts that the new locks will work well.

7. Children get bumps when they test their limits.

8. The stylist lifts her locks with a comb before she cuts her hair.

9. Chris writes and recites poetry.

10. The woman steps carefully over the spots where there are water leaks.

CD 3:25

2. **Final <u>voiced</u> consonants**, (/b/, /d/, /g/, /v/, "th" or /ð/, /m/, /n/, /l/, /r/, /w/, "y" or /j/), and vowels, add a /z/ sound, as follows:

rub**s**	rod**s**	dog**s**
wave**s**	breathe**s**	form**s**
win**s**	call**s**	cow**s**

Exercise 3: Practice reading the following words aloud. Make sure that you pronounce the **-s** as a /z/ sound when the last sound heard in the root word is voiced.

degrees	blows	dries
employs	denies	grows
pays	knees	series
says	draws	chews
clues	buys	ties
toys	tables	razors
raisins	wives	husbands
slabs	clubs	dogs

Exercise 4: Underline the final /z/ sound in the following sentences and say them aloud. Remember to link the words together.

1. *My company employs good workers and pays them well.*

2. *The tables were made of slabs of granite.*

3. *The dull razors cut her knees when she shaved.*

4. *All of her former boyfriends were afraid of dogs.*

5. Kayla buys raisins for the children.

6. The wives bought golf clubs for their husbands' birthdays.

7. Sharon grows and dries flowers to make lovely glass picture frames.

8. Harriet ties bows on her little girl's braids.

9. Bill says the clues do not solve the crimes.

10. Alice ties yellow ribbons around the trees.

---

3. *Words ending in /s/, /z/, "sh" or /ʃ/, "ch" or /tʃ/, "zh" or /ʒ/, and "j" or /dʒ/, add the -ez suffix. This suffix becomes a separate syllable and sounds like "-ez" or [əz].*

| *stresses* | *encloses* | *wishes* |
| watches | garages | judges |

Exercise 5: Practice reading the following words. Make sure that you pronounce the **-s** ending as an "-ez" [əz] suffix when the last sound in the word is /s/, /z/, "sh" or /ʃ /, "ch" or /tʃ/, "zh" or /ʒ], or "j" or /dʒ/.

dresses	possesses	leases
erases	places	impresses
stresses	expresses	revitalizes
reduces	bonuses	focuses
prices	reverses	closes
eases	pleases	squeezes
amazes	praises	uses
loses	accuses	disposes
washes	dishes	crashes
matches	badges	edges

Exercise 6: Underline the final **-s** or [-əz] in the following sentences and say them aloud. Remember to link the words together.

1. *The prices of the designer dresses are ridiculously expensive.*

2. *Melanie uses tubes of toothpaste and squeezes them from the bottom.*

3. *The cream that Charlotte uses reduces the signs of aging.*

4. *Karin possesses leases to several houses at the beach.*

5. It amazes Rita how much her mother praises her accomplishments.

6. Yoga eases Marjorie's stresses and revitalizes her energy.

7. Ana expresses disappointment when she loses in chess matches.

8. Zak sneezes when he sleeps in dusty places.

9. It pleases Larry when he closes deals and receives unexpected bonuses.

10. It impresses me when Jayden disposes newspapers in the recycle bin.

21. Consonant Blends and Clusters

*Consonant blends and clusters occur at the beginning, middle, and end of words. It is important to pronounce all of the sounds, but you do **NOT** insert a break between the sounds. For example, say "please," not "puh-lease."*

When you pronounce consonant blends, the letters are influenced by the adjacent sounds, so that you say it with stronger or weaker voicing than if you pronounce it alone. For example, "corre**ct**" vs. "ne**t**"," "**sp**ort," vs. "**p**ort", "sen**t**" vs. "se**t**."

Sometimes, some of the final clusters may become reduced in conversation to allow the sentence to flow smoothly.

> *He was the firs~~t~~ one.*
> *Please pass the cream an~~d~~ sugar.*

CD 4:1

Exercise 1: Say the followings words and remember to pronounce the blend or consonant cluster correctly. Look up the meanings of the unfamiliar words to increase your vocabulary. Words with multiple meanings and/or multiple parts of speech are shown with a star (★). Then, make up a sentence or write a definition for the words you don't know. Finally, practice saying the sentences aloud and focus on the consonant blends or clusters. Add your own personal vocabulary words to each section.

A. INITIAL "R" BLENDS

Initial /br/ blends

CD 4:2

break★	breadth★	browser
breakfast	bridge★	brand★
browse	brief★	broken★
breath★	brilliant★	brainstorm
bribery	brunch	bridal/bridle★

Sentences and/or definitions:

1._____

```
┌─────────────────────────────────────────────────────────────┐
│ ┌─────────────────────────────────────────────────────────┐ │
│ │ 2._____   │ │
│ │                                                         │ │
│ │ Personal Words:                                         │ │
│ └─────────────────────────────────────────────────────────┘ │
└─────────────────────────────────────────────────────────────┘
```

Exercise 2: Read aloud the sentences containing words with consonant blends or clusters. You may know additional meanings for some of these words. The highlighted words from the list can have different meanings depending upon the context. Try to you identifying and/or defining the various meanings?

NOTE: Be careful not to automatically stress the word in the bold. It is not always the most important word.

Break
1. *Be careful; if you drop the glass vial, it will **break**.*
2. Mariel wanted to **break** the record for most saves during a soccer game.
3. Getting a big account was a lucky **break** for the young business owner.
4. Let's take a **break** since we've been working so hard all afternoon.
5. He didn't want to **break** the law, so he refused to carry out his bosses' instructions.
6. Anne was afraid she would **break** under the school's pressure.
7. Susan promised not to **break** her promises.
8. She thought her heart would **break** when they got divorced.
9. Her skin will **break** out if she eats greasy food.

Breath
1. *Take a deep **breath** and relax.*
2. Open the window so we can get a **breath** of fresh, ocean air.
3. He brushes his teeth to eliminate his bad **breath**.

Brilliant
1. *Albert Einstein was a **brilliant** scholar.*
2. Is her engagement ring an emerald or **brilliant** cut?
3. The **brilliant** sunshine was welcomed after all the rain.

Bridge
1. *Charlotte and Jack play **bridge** with their friends every Friday evening.*
2. The George Washington **Bridge** crosses the Hudson River.
3. The dentist affixed a **bridge** to her patient's molars.
4. Katie hurt the **bridge** of her nose playing softball.
5. The violin strings are attached to the **bridge** of the instrument.

Brief
1. *The detective was instructed to **brief** his task force.*
2. This meeting has to be **brief** because I am expecting an overseas call.
3. Michelle carried her **brief** into the courtroom.

Breadth
1. *I didn't realize the **breadth** of this commitment.*

2. Can you measure the **breadth** of this office?

Bridle/Bridal
1. *The acting coach didn't want to **bridle** his students' enthusiasm, despite their lack of talent.*
2. Can you please put that horse's **bridle** in the barn?
3. The **bridal** party wore lavender dresses.

Brand
1. *The cattle rancher needed to **brand** his cows so they could be identified.*
2. What is your favorite **brand** of toothpaste?
3. In advertising, it is important to **brand** yourself so people recognize your business.

Broken
1. *My grandmother spoke **broken** English when she first came to America.*
2. Our phone connection was **broken** during the storm.
3. The antique porcelain doll's face was **broken**.
4. She suffered a **broken** heart after the break-up.

Initial /pr/ blends

CD
4:3

print ★	proud ★	prize ★
prove	proof ★	prestige
predominant	preview ★	president
privacy	promise ★	profit ★
promotion	pressure ★	primary ★
privilege ★	product	pronounce

Sentences and/or definitions:

1._____

2._____

Personal words:

Print
1. *The artist signed this limited-edition **print**.*
2. Do you like the **print** on this scarf?
3. Please **print** your name neatly on the line.
4. We can make a **print** from this old negative.

Privilege

1. *Chase lost a **privilege** when he didn't come in the house when his mother called him.*
2. Meyer thought it was an honor and a **privilege** to serve in the Navy.
3. Children of **privilege** attended the posh boarding school.

Proof

1. *You must give me **proof** that she tried to steal my jewelry.*
2. This vodka is 90 **proof**.
3. Mike completed the difficult **proof** in geometry class.

Preview

1. *The entertainment critic went to the movie **preview** two days before it was released.*
2. The designer will **preview** her designs during Fall Fashion week in New York City.

Pressure

1. *I will not sign this contract under **pressure**.*
2. Please apply **pressure** to this wound to stop the bleeding.
3. The atmospheric **pressure** drops before a storm.

Prize

1. *What qualities do you **prize** in a person?*
2. Let's put your **prize** in the display cabinet.
3. He entered his **prize** hog in the state fair competition.

Primary

1. *What is your **primary** goal for this course?*
2. Remember to vote in the **primary** election.
3. Is blue a **primary** color?

Profit

1. *How much of a **profit** do you think you will make from the sale of the house?*
2. We could all **profit** from a day off.

Proud

1. *I am **proud** of your accomplishments.*
2. Her aunt was a **proud** and arrogant woman.

Promise

1. *I **promise** to reserve two tickets for you at the door.*
2. It isn't nice to break a **promise**.

Initial /dr/ blends

drink★	*drapes ★*	*drive ★*
drowsy	*drill ★*	*draft ★*
dream★	drastically	dripping
drizzling	drenched	dreaded
drawing ★	*drug ★*	dressing ★

Sentences and/or definitions:

1._____

2._____

Personal words:

Drapes
1. *The **drapes** were hung with velvet sashes.*
2. That dress **drapes** nicely in the back.

Draft
1. *Please close the window; I am getting a cold **draft**.*
2. We haven't finished the formatting; this is just a rough **draft**.
3. The **draft** horses can haul the wagon.
4. The bar serves **draft** and bottled beer.
5. He moved to Canada to avoid the **draft**.

Drawing
1. *Lynda has been **drawing** large audiences at her speaking engagements.*
2. Alex likes **drawing** with colored pencils.
3. He's been **drawing** money out of their savings account.
4. Susanne greeted the guest in the **drawing** room.

Drink
1. *May I get you a cold **drink**?*
2. I want to **drink** in the aroma of the fragrant flowers.
3. I'll **drink** a glass of wine with dinner.

Drug
1. *This **drug** was recently approved by the FDA.*
2. Don't forget to pick up the prescription at the **drug** store.
3. There was mandatory illicit **drug** testing of the Olympic athletes.

Dressing
1. *Mary is **dressing** the turkey for the Thanksgiving dinner.*
2. The nurse changed the patient's **dressing**.
3. Jayden is still **dressing** for the gala ball.

Drill
1. *Can you help me **drill** these screws into the shelf?*
2. I need to **drill** these pronunciation rules into my head!
3. The teacher gave the students a math **drill** every Thursday.
4. I am afraid of the dentist's **drill**.
5. The **drill** sergeant offered no sympathy to the tired soldiers.

Drive
1. *I can **drive** you to the theater.*
2. Will turned to his golfing buddy and said, "Nice **drive**!"
3. It is dangerous to drink and **drive**.
4. His repeated questions will **drive** me crazy!
5. Jeremy participated in the canned goods **drive** to help the homeless.

Dream
1. *Do you **dream** in color?*
2. Her wedding gown is a **dream** in chiffon and lace.

Initial /tr/ blends

---

trip ★	try ★	trick ★
tray	trees	trial ★
truth	trustworthy	trap ★
treat ★	triplicate	treasurer
transfer ★	trauma	trust ★

CD 4:5

Sentences and/or definitions:

1._____

2._____

Personal Words:

Trip
1. *Janie, Jean, and Marjorie are planning a **trip** to Key Biscayne.*
2. Be careful; I don't want you to **trip** on that scatter rug.
3. The thieves were trying not to **trip** the sophisticated security alarm.

©2006, RULES

Treat

1. *Would you like a sweet **treat** for your afternoon snack?*
2. Put your wallet away; it's my **treat**.
3. How is the doctor planning to **treat** her painful symptoms?
4. I know that she will **treat** her guests with kindness.
5. The children exclaimed, "Trick or **Treat**" on Halloween.

Transfer

1. *When you change busses, remember to ask for a **transfer**.*
2. Sharon has decided to **transfer** to another college.
3. Michele will **transfer** the pattern onto the fabric.

Try

1. *The judge will **try** the case in criminal court.*
2. It doesn't matter if you can't skate well; just give it a **try**!
3. I always **try** to do my best.

Trick

1. *The magician did my favorite **trick**.*
2. The salesman tried to **trick** me into buying parts that I didn't need.

Trial

1. *The accused men went on **trial** last Monday.*
2. When will the results of the clinical **trial** be released?
3. They did a **trial** run to make it easier when they drove to the interview on Tuesday.

Trap

1. *The mouse was caught in a **trap**.*
2. We got caught in his **trap** of deceit.
3. They will **trap** the bear when he gets close to the campsite.

Trust

1. *I **trust** you implicitly.*
2. The minor's assets were placed in a **trust** fund.

Initial /kr/ blends

creative	crooked	crush ★
cream ★	creek/creak ★	create
crack ★	crowded	crime
crimson	criticize	credible
chrome	crash ★	crisis

CD 4:6

Cream
1. *Does this soup have a broth or **cream** base?*
2. Do you use a moisturizing lotion or **cream**?
3. Are her sheets white or **cream**?
4. Lee likes **cream** cheese on her bagel.
5. The first step in preparing cookie dough is to **cream** the butter and sugar together.

Crack
1. *I heard the branch **crack** when I stepped on it.*
2. Janie decided to take a **crack** at tennis.
3. We can't use this teacup because it has a **crack** in it.
4. The drug addict was arrested for possession of **crack** cocaine.
5. Maddy will **crack** up when she hears this story!

Crash
1. *There was a terrible car **crash** in front of our house.*
2. I don't want to **crash** the party without an invitation.
3. I would like take a **crash** course in web design.
4. Did you see Bill **crash** into the street sign?

Crush
1. *There was a **crush** of people at the gates of the stadium.*
2. I need to **crush** these flax seeds.
3. Sasha has a **crush** on Lucas, who has blue eyes and blonde hair.

Creek/Creak
1. *Let's sit down by the **creek** and have our picnic.*
2. What do you know about the **Creek** Indians from the southern part of the United States?
3. The old floorboards **creak** as I walk over them.
4. I heard a **creak** as I climbed up the stairs.

CD 4:7

green ★	growth ★	grave ★
grip ★	greeting	graduation
greatest	grammar	grandparent
grueling	grind ★	ground ★
group ★	grade ★	graceful

Sentences and/or definitions:

1._____

2._____

Personal Words:

Green

1. *Andrea has lovely **green** eyes.*
2. You might get a stomach ache if you eat **green** fruit before it is ripe.
3. If you support **green** issues, you may want to purchase a hybrid car.
4. The intern is **green** at performing certain procedures.
5. You better lie down; you look **green** around the gills.

Grip

1. *You should shake hands with a firm **grip**.*
2. I need to replace the **grip** on my tennis racket.
3. Some men don't have a **grip** on women's issues.
4. **Grip** the heavy jug with both hands.
5. The impatient teenager said, "Get a **grip**!"

Group

1. *How many people are in our **group**?*
2. Let's **group** these cards according to size.

Growth

1. *He had to have a small **growth** on his hand surgically removed.*
2. She has had a **growth** spurt.
3. His mutual fund showed a lot of **growth** in the last quarter.

Grind

1. *Let's **grind** the spices just before putting them in the stew.*
2. If you work all the time, you may feel like you are in a **grind**.
3. Do you **grind** your teeth when you sleep?

Grade
1. *She got a passing **grade** in her most demanding class.*
2. That country road has a steep **grade**.
3. They have 25 children in their first **grade** class.

Grave
1. *They will put flowers on the **grave** of their ancestors.*
2. The doctor discussed the **grave** medical condition.

Ground
1. *The **ground** is very wet after all of the recent rain.*
2. How do you **ground** these electrical currents?
3. They are required to pay **ground** rent when they purchase a new house.

Initial /fr/ blends

CD 4:8

friend	freeze ★	fry ★
frame ★	frank	fruit
freedom	fresh ★	fragile
free ★	Friday	front ★
frown ★	frequent	freelance

Sentences and/or definitions:

1. _____

2. _____

Personal Words:

Frame
1. *What size picture **frame** do you need?*
2. What is the best way to **frame** the proposal?
3. According to the book, it appears she is trying to **frame** him for the crime.

Free
1. *Museum entrance is **free** on the last Wednesday of the month.*
2. Since I live alone, I am **free** to make my own social plans.
3. I am **free** after 6 p.m. on Tuesday.
4. The young girl was a **free**-sprit.

Freeze
1. *The flowers will **freeze** if you leave them on the porch tonight.*
2. I am afraid I will **freeze** when I see them together.

©2006, RULES

3. The company placed a **freeze** on hiring new employees.
4. The nervous speaker worried that she would **freeze** during her presentation.

Fresh
1. *The bread at the bakery is made **fresh** every morning.*
2. Daria felt **fresh** after her long nap.
3. The teenager was **fresh** to his parents.
4. Let's get a **fresh** start on our road trip.

Front
1. *Do you button this blouse in the back or in the **front**?*
2. Is this business a **front** for the mob?
3. The weather channel predicted a cold **front** from Canada this week.

Fry
1. *Should I **fry** the fish or broil it?*
2. In Gloucester, Massachusetts you can find lots of fish **fry** at the local fisheries.
3. If you stay out in the hot sun too long, you will **fry**.

Frown
1. *Some people **frown** when they are perplexed.*
2. When Alice took the photograph, Daria had a **frown** on her face.

Initial /thr/ blends

---

throw ★	throat	throttle ★
thread ★	three	through/threw ★
thrifty	threaten	thrilled
throb	threshold ★	thruway
thrive ★	throng	throughout ★

Sentences and/or definitions:

1._____

2._____

Personal Words:

CD 4:9

Throw
1. *Sasha can **throw** the ball very well.*
2. Kathleen knit a beautiful **throw** for the bed.
3. Just **throw** on a jacket and let's go!
4. I don't want to play basketball with you if you intend to **throw** the game.
5. It is hard to **throw** the car into fifth gear.
6. You don't need a sweater, but a lightweight **throw** might be appropriate.

7. Fatima likes to **throw** herself into the character she is portraying.
8. When someone has a stomach virus, he may **throw** up.

Thread
1. *May I borrow a needle and **thread** to fix this jacket?*
2. Can you follow the **thread** of this e-mail?
3. **Thread** it through the eye of the needle.

Thrive
1. *I am sure their business will **thrive** once they get the money from the investors.*
2. The baby will **thrive** on her mother's milk.

Threshold
1. *What is your **threshold** for pain?*
2. The groom carried his bride across the **threshold**.

Throttle
1. The driver choked up on the **throttle**.
2. You can give me a hug, but don't **throttle** me!

Through
1. *They work Monday **through** Friday.*
2. Can you see **through** this material?
3. Ted is **through** with carpentry projects.
4. Is this a **through** street or a dead end?
5. Let's drive **through** the tunnel.

Throughout
1. *The baby cried **throughout** the entire movie.*
2. There is trash **throughout** the park.

Initial /skr/ blends

CD
4:10

scrap ★	scrape ★	screen ★
screwdriver ★	scream ★	scrambling ★
screening ★	scribble	scrabble
scratch ★	scroll ★	scrutinize
scruples	scrupulous	script ★

Sentences and/or definitions:

1._____

2._____

Personal Words:

©2006, RULES

Scrap

1. *May I have a **scrap** of paper to write down your phone number?*
2. Lois wanted a **scrap** book for her memoirs.
3. The managers decided to **scrap** the idea.

Screwdriver

1. *There should be a **screwdriver** in my tool box.*
2. The bartender mixed vodka and orange juice to make a **screwdriver**.

Screening

1. *There will be a **screening** of all new student films during the month of January.*
2. Wendy conducted a hearing **screening** on all newborns at the hospital.
3. They are **screening** the children for speech difficulties.

Scratch

1. *Amanda got a **scratch** on her leg when she fell in the playground.*
2. She made the cookies from **scratch**.
3. They decided to **scratch** their original vacation plans.
4. After years of practice, Larry became a **scratch** golfer.

Scrape

1. *Let's all **scrape** some money together to buy them a nice gift.*
2. I got a **scrape** on my hand from the cheese grater.
3. I had to **scrape** the ice off the windshield of my car.

Scroll

1. *Please **scroll** to the bottom of your computer screen.*
2. The **scroll** was made of parchment.

Screen

1. *There is a small tear in the window **screen**.*
2. There is a decorative **screen** in the bedroom.
3. Is there a scratch on the TV **screen**?
4. Jeff's secretary will **screen** his calls.

Scrambling

1. *Everyone is **scrambling** for a good seat at the movie theater.*
2. Evie is in the kitchen **scrambling** eggs.

Script

1. *The actors auctioned off a signed **script** from their hit television show for a charity.*
2. She signed her name in **script** with a flourish.

Scream

1. *Alex will **scream** if he finds a spider in his room.*
2. Did you hear that awful **scream** in the middle of the night?

CD
4:11

spring★	spray★	spread★
sprawl★	spry	sprig
sprint	spruce★	sprout★
sprite★	spree	sprained

Sentences and/or definitions:

1._____

2._____

Personal Words:

Sprout
1. *I pulled the single bean **sprout** from the salad.*
2. He will **sprout** up over the summer.

Sprawl
1. *I'm going to **sprawl** out on this big towel at the beach.*
2. A town meeting was held to discuss the issue of urban **sprawl.**

Spring
1. *The flowers bloom in the **spring.***
2. **Spring** out of the classroom as soon as you can.
3. Bill offered to **spring** for dinner.
4. Did you buy a foam or a **spring** mattress?

Spray
1. ***Spray** the plants with pesticide once a month.*
2. I need a new can of hair **spray.**
3. They included a **spray** of baby's breath in the floral arrangement.

Spread
1. ***Spread** the strawberry jam on the toast.*
2. The professor stated that there was a huge **spread** in the grades on that test.
3. **Spread** the wings apart on the wounded bird.
4. Germs **spread** quickly in dirty environments.
5. Shannon will **spread** all of the photographs out before she puts them in the album.

Sprite
1. *The old widower was still handsome and **sprite.***
2. Could you pick up some Pepsi® and **Sprite®** at the supermarket?

©2006, RULES

3. Elana wrote a story about a **sprite** and goblin with magical powers.

Spruce
1. *We have a lovely **spruce** in our backyard.*
2. Do you have any decorating ideas to **spruce** up the family room?

Initial /shr/ blends

CD
4:12

shred ★	shriek	shrimp ★
shrub	shrugged	shrine
shrink ★	shroud	shrivel
shrewd	shrill	shrinkage

Sentences and/or definitions:

1._____

2._____

Personal Words:

Shrimp
1. *Can you please buy a pound of frozen **shrimp**?*
2. Kim's nickname is **shrimp** because she is so short.

Shrink
1. *Shy people tend to **shrink** in front of an audience.*
2. A psychiatrist can be called a "**shrink**."
3. Your shirt will **shrink** if you wash it in hot water.

Shred
1. *Make sure to **shred** all of the documents.*
2. He didn't have a **shred** of evidence to solve the crime.

Initial /str/ blends

CD
4:13

straw ★	string ★	street
stripe ★	strap ★	strand ★
stray ★	strawberry	straddle ★
streak ★	strict	straighten

Straw

1. *She wore a lovely **straw** hat with a black velvet ribbon.*
2. The horse grazed on **straw** in the afternoon sun.
3. We drank our ice cream sodas through a **straw**.

Streak

1. *Did you see that **streak** of lightning?*
2. There was a bright **streak** of color in the painting.
3. Susan wants to **streak** her hair blonde.

String

1. *Have you ever eaten **string** cheese?*
2. How long can he **string** her along before he gives an answer?
3. She wanted a **string** of pearls for her birthday.
4. We tied the package with colorful **string**.
5. What **string** instrument does William play?

Stress

1. *Sally is undergoing a great deal of **stress** at her job.*
2. How do you **stress** an important word in a sentence?
3. I will try to **stress** my point using PowerPoint® slides and video clips.
4. Don't **stress** over the test results.

Strand

1. *He put a **strand** of her hair in a locket.*
2. The jewelry designer used a thick **strand** of silk to make the necklace.
3. Don't **strand** me out in the cold.

Straddle

1. *The politician tried to **straddle** the controversial issue.*
2. Annie stretched her hamstrings by sitting in a **straddle** position on the floor.
3. Jake will **straddle** the horse at the ranch.

Stray

1. *We rescued a **stray** cat from the animal shelter.*
2. Please don't **stray** too far from the campsite or you might get lost.

Strap

1. *This old steamer trunk has a leather **strap** across the top.*

2. The **strap** of my sundress is torn.
3. Please **strap** this package to the roof rack of the car.

Stripe
1. *The police officer earned a **stripe** after ten years of service.*
2. This flag has a large red **stripe**.

B. INITIAL "L" BLENDS

Initial /bl/ blends

bleeding	blaze	blight
blown	black ★	blue ★
bleach ★	blizzard	block ★
blueprint	blurry	blackmail
blackout	blanket ★	bland

Sentences and/or definitions:

1._____

2._____

Personal Words:

CD
4:14

Bleach
1. *You can whiten your laundry with **bleach**.*
2. Dentists offer a lot of techniques to **bleach** your teeth.
3. In the winter, she likes to **bleach** her hair blonde.

Black
1. *Her hair was as **black** as a raven.*
2. The author's stories were **black** and ominous.
3. The Caribbean Islands are known for **black** magic.
4. The accountant reported that the company was in the **black**.

Blanket
1. *Their **blanket** was made out of wool.*
2. They had a **blanket** insurance policy for every member of their household.
3. A **blanket** of snow covered the field.

Blue
1. *The American flag is red, white, and **blue**.*
2. Janya was **blue** when her best friend moved away.

Block
1. *This toy **block** has an "M" written on it.*
2. On which city **block** do they live?
3. The delivery truck shouldn't be allowed to **block** the driveway.
4. Let's **block** out three days for the conference.
5. We have a **block** party scheduled for the 4th of July.
6. I will **block** your move.
7. Let's **block** out the dance steps before we rehearse.
8. What is going up next on the auction **block**?

Initial /pl/ blends

CD
4:15

please★	plow	place ★
plight	pleated	placement
plastic	plural	plunged
pliers	pleasing	plus ★
platform★	platter	plunger

Sentences and/or definitions:

1._____

2._____

Personal Words:

Please
1. *Saying **please** and thank-you is a sign of good manners.*
2. The hostess wanted to **please** her guests.

Platform
1. *The Democrats and Republicans announced their **platform** at the convention.*
2. The students approached the **platform** to receive their diplomas.
3. She wore **platform** shoes to make herself look taller.

Place
1. *Is there a **place** for all of these books?*
2. Where did Beth **place** in the competition?
3. I don't want to **place** a bet.
4. **Place** the diploma in a prominent spot.

Plus
1. *One **plus** one equals two.*
2. They will have cake **plus** ice cream at the party.
3. After she gained so much weight, she had to wear **plus** sizes.

©2006, RULES

Initial /kl/ blends

chlorine	clown	closet ★
class ★	clarity	client
cleft ★	clock ★	clue
clean ★	click/clique ★	clarify
clerical	clash ★	closure ★

Sentences and/or definitions:

1._____

2._____

Personal Words:

CD
4:16

Class
1. *My mother has a lot of **class**.*
2. There are thirty children in her **class**.
3. Some cultures have a **class** system.

Clean
1. *Jai-Lee has a very **clean** home.*
2. I have to **clean** every room in this house!
3. The doctor made a **clean** incision.
4. The politician's reputation was **clean**.
5. The politician won with a **clean** sweep of Illinois.
6. Phil received a **clean** bill of health.

Clock
1. *Do you have an alarm **clock**?*
2. Russ wanted to **clock** his best time in the marathon this year.
3. The factory workers had to **clock** in and **clock** out every day.

Click/clique
1. *Did you hear a **click** when you opened the door?*
2. I want to introduce my sister to your brother because I think they will really **click**.
3. The popular girls formed a **clique** in their high school.

Clash
1. *I don't want to **clash** with you on the party plans.*
2. The cymbals made a loud **clash**!
3. The plaid and print patterns **clash**.

Closet
1. *My **closet** is too small and cluttered.*
2. He decided to come out of the **closet** instead of keeping secrets any longer.

Closure
1. *My winter coat has a toggle **closure**.*
2. After being estranged from her mother for years, Barbara wanted to have **closure** before she died.

Cleft
1. *The baby was born with a **cleft** palate.*
2. Some people find a **cleft** of the chin very attractive.

Initial /gl/ blends

4:17

gloss★	glare ★	glass ★
glowing	glad ★	glory
gleam ★	glitter ★	glacier
glossary	glow ★	glider ★
glaze	glib	glucose

Sentences and/or definitions:

1._____

2._____

Personal Words:

Gloss
1. *Her hair has a lovely **gloss**.*
2. What color lip **gloss** should I wear?
3. Please don't **gloss** over the details of the assignment.

Gleam
1. *There was a sparkly **gleam** in her eyes.*
2. We had a **gleam** of hope that everything would work out fine.

Glare
1. *Martha turned and looked at them with a harsh **glare**.*
2. It was hard to drive because of the afternoon **glare**.

Glow
1. *There was a nice, warm **glow** emanating from the hearth.*
2. Her cheeks had a rosy **glow**.

Glass

1. *This is an old-fashioned **glass** milk bottle.*
2. Fill the **glass** with water, please.

Glider

1. *We went to the airfield to watch the beautiful **glider**.*
2. We have a **glider** hanging from the ceiling of our front porch that seats four people.

Glitter

1. *The gold ring will **glitter** in the sunlight.*
2. Suzy wore **glitter** on her face for the recital.

Glad

1. *I am **glad** that you can come to my party.*
2. I would be **glad** to volunteer for the committee.

Initial /fl/ blends

float★	flatten	fluctuation
flight★	flown	flow charts
fluid★	flake ★	floor ★
flexible	flashlight	flammable
floppy ★	floss ★	fluency

Sentences and/or definitions:

1._____

2._____

Personal Words:

Float

1. *Will this bottle **float** in the water?*
2. The bank officer decided to **float** us the loan.
3. Which was your favorite **float** in the Thanksgiving Day Parade?
4. Mike ordered a root beer **float**.

Flight

1. *What time is your **flight** expected to arrive?*
2. Our psychology class studied the fight or **flight** response to stress.
3. The birds took **flight** when the fireworks began.

Fluid

1. *Patrick poured the **fluid** from one vial to another.*

2. The political situation is still **fluid** in that country.
3. The ballet dancer's moves are graceful and **fluid**.

Floppy
1. *My dog has **floppy** ears.*
2. Where should I store this **floppy** disc?

Flake
1. *Who discovered that every **flake** of snow is different?*
2. I may be forgetful, but I am not a **flake**.
3. The filet of sole will **flake** when it is done cooking.

Floss
1. *I am supposed to **floss** my teeth three times a day.*
2. Would you please buy some dental **floss** at the pharmacy?
3. This beautiful dress is embroidered with silver and gold **floss**.

Floor
1. *This parquet **floor** is beautiful.*
2. The senator strode to the **floor**.
3. The singer will **floor** you with her high notes!
4. The young boy told his Dad to **floor** it while driving on the causeway.

C. INITIAL "S" BLENDS

Initial /sl/ blends

sleep★	slim ★	slipper
slate ★	slender	slant★
sloppy	slope ★	slowly
slurp	slump★	slice ★
slightly	slap ★	slurring

Sentences and/or definitions:

1._____

2._____

Personal Words:

CD
4:19

Sleep
1. Does your boat **sleep** six or eight people?
2. What time do you usually go to **sleep**?
3. I plan to **sleep** late today.
4. The child woke up from a nap and had **sleep** in her eyes.

©2006, RULES

Slate

1. *That house has a **slate** roof.*
2. What's on the **slate** for today's meeting?
3. Let's start out with a clean **slate**.

Slim

1. *Most models are tall and **slim**.*
2. I think that law has a **slim** chance of passing the legislature.
3. They sold **Slim** Jim's™ at the truck stop.

Slope

1. *What is the **slope** of that angle?*
2. Have you ever skied that **slope** before?
3. She needs to get some counseling as she is on a slippery **slope** these days.

Slump

1. *When you **slump** in your chair, it is bad for your posture.*
2. These sales projections have everyone in a **slump** at the office.

Slap

1. *Her rude remark was quite a **slap** to her boss.*
2. The boys were told not to **slap** or punch!

Slice

1. *Would you like me to **slice** the pie?*
2. I'll have a small **slice** of the cake.
3. The tennis pro showed us how to **slice** the ball.

Slant

1. *The talk show host presented the news with his own political **slant**.*
2. The boardwalk to the beach is on a slight **slant**.

Initial /spl/ blends

---

splash ★	splinter	splendid
splurge	splotchy	splatter
splitting ★	spleen	splint

CD 4:20

Sentences and/or definitions:

1._____

2._____

Personal Words:

Splash

1. *The kids like to **splash** around in the ocean.*
2. The dish made a **splash** when it was dropped in the sink.

Splitting

1. *Jay was **splitting** the wood with an axe.*
2. Michele had a **splitting** headache after spending the day outside.
3. Are you **splitting** up the prizes between the two children?
4. Risa and Jake are **splitting** up.

Initial /sp/ blends

CD
4:21

Spanish	spare ★	spill ★
speech ★	specialized	speakers ★
speed ★	spin ★	space ★
spend ★	spirits ★	spontaneous
spectrum ★	specific	spatial

Sentences and/or definitions:

1._____

2._____

Personal Words:

Speech

1. *The student was anxious about giving her **speech** to the class.*
2. Lori has to go to **speech** therapy.

Speed

1. *What is the **speed** limit in town?*
2. You need to shift the bike's **speed** when climbing a steep hill.
3. The officials clocked the **speed** of the athlete's serve.
4. The drug dealer sold crack cocaine and **speed**.

Spend

1. *How much would you like to **spend** on the holiday gifts?*
2. I can **spend** two hours on our project this afternoon.

Spectrum

1. *When you look through a prism, you can see all of the lights of the **spectrum**.*
2. There is a wide **spectrum** of opinion concerning that political issue.

Spare

1. *Please keep the **spare** tire in the trunk of the car.*
2. Can you **spare** some time this weekend to help me around the house?
3. James got a **spare** the first time he went bowling.
4. I will **spare** you the embarrassment and do it myself.
5. I have to go food shopping because our provisions are **spare**.

Spin

1. *Have you ever tried a **spin** class at your gym?*
2. The Public Relations Department will put a **spin** on the news reports.
3. You may get dizzy if you **spin** around like that.
4. A spider can **spin** a web quickly.
5. Can you please **spin** this yarn for me?
6. I'd like to take the bike out for a **spin** around the park.

Spirits

1. *The package store sells wines and **spirits**.*
2. Mary Rose was in good **spirits** after she made partner in her law firm.
3. They talked about evil **spirits** on Halloween.
4. Kennedy High School had a pep rally to raise school **spirit**.

Spill

1. *An oil **spill** can cause a great deal of damage to wildlife and the environment.*
2. Hold this bowl with both hands so that it won't **spill**.
3. Amanda took a bad **spill** off of her bicycle.

Speakers

1. *The electrician installed **speakers** in the ceiling.*
2. The **speakers** were interesting and dynamic.

Space

1. *Do you have **space** for all of your shoes?*
2. The astronauts live and work in **space**.
3. Please leave **space** between the stories for editorial comments.
4. Can you save a **space** for me on the train?
5. Lacey's girlfriends called her a **space** cadet.

Initial /st/ blends

CD
4:22

stand ★	stay ★	static ★
storage	staff ★	statistic
statement ★	start ★	stock ★
steal/steel ★	station ★	status ★
stake/steak ★	stack ★	stare/stair ★

Sentences and/or definitions:

1._____

2._____

Personal Words:

Stand
1. *Let's meet at the taxi **stand**.*
2. Marjorie can't **stand** the smell of nail polish.
3. What does this symbol **stand** for?
4. I can **stand** if there are no more seats available.
5. Please put this African Violet on the **stand** in the corner.
6. Can you please buy some strawberries at the farm **stand**?
7. There is some sheet music on the **stand** in the music room.
8. Lorraine and Milt saw a **stand**-up comic at the comedy club.

Statement
1. *The auditor looked at the **statement** with a concerned look on his face.*
2. The President issued a **statement** this morning.
3. The interior designer helped make a **statement** when you entered the foyer.

Steal/steel
1. *It is wrong to **steal** something from a store.*
2. Would you like to **steal** away for the afternoon?
3. I know that player is going to try to **steal** second base.
4. The **steel** beams supported the building.
5. The sword was made of **steel**.

Stake/steak
1. *I have to hammer one more **stake** and the tent will be ready.*
2. I wouldn't **stake** my life on it!
3. The witches were burned at the **stake** during the Salem witch hunts.
4. The police officers set up a **stake**-out to catch the criminals.
5. Let's put some **steak** on the grill for dinner.

152   ©2006, RULES

Stay

1. *The obedient dog followed the command to "stay."*
2. You are welcome to **stay** a little longer.
3. We had a nice **stay** in Tuscany last year.
4. The governor approved a **stay** of execution for the criminal.

Staff

1. *The mountain climber carried a **staff**.*
2. Bread is considered to be the **staff** of life.
3. Can you read the notes on a musical **staff**?
4. How can we **staff** the office in just two weeks?
5. We hired some temporary **staff** for the busy holiday rush.

Start

1. *When does the movie **start**?*
2. Jack woke with a **start** from his nap.
3. I will **start** getting ready after lunch.

Station

1. *I can drive you home from the **station**.*
2. What is her **station** in life?
3. The TV **station** has expensive and sophisticated equipment.
4. At this catering **station**, you can get coffee and dessert.

Static

1. *Unfortunately, there is a lot of **static** electricity on the line.*
2. I can't hear you. There is too much **static**.
3. The **static** community did not change with the times.

Status

1. *What is the **status** of the project you have been working on?*
2. With his new promotion, he had an elevated **status** at the company.
3. The patient's neurological **status** was fluctuating.

Stock

1. *In colonial days, prisoners were placed in a **stock** for public humiliation.*
2. If you are looking for Jim, he is unloading boxes in the **stock** room.
3. We received notification that there was a **stock** split, so we now have twice as many shares.
4. Ann was going to be in summer **stock** theatre in upstate New York.
5. Russ prepared a vegetable **stock** for his risotto dinner.

Stack

1. *Would you like maple syrup on your **stack** of pancakes?*
2. Be careful not to **stack** the dishes too high.
3. It would be unfair to **stack** your team with the best players.

Stare/Stair

1. *The bottom **stair** is broken, so be careful!*
2. It is impolite to **stare** at someone.

3. She gave the teacher a blank **stare**.

Initial /sn/ blends

<table>
<tr><td>snap ★</td><td>snip</td><td>snide</td></tr>
<tr><td>snow★</td><td>snug</td><td>snag ★</td></tr>
<tr><td>snake★</td><td>sneeze ★</td><td>sneak</td></tr>
<tr><td>snob</td><td>snub</td><td>snore</td></tr>
<tr><td>snare</td><td>snarl★</td><td>snoop</td></tr>
</table>

Sentences and/or definitions:

1._____

2._____

Personal Words:

CD
4:23

Snap
1. *I can get ready in a **snap**.*
2. Please stand still so Alice can **snap** your photo.
3. The strap on my sandal is so old, I am afraid it will **snap** off.
4. Would you like to eat some sugar **snap** peas?
5. We had a cold **snap** last week.
6. Can you help me close the top **snap** of my dress?

Snow
1. ***Snow** is predicted overnight.*
2. Do you think it will **snow** this evening?
3. Our cable went out and all I can see on the TV is **snow**.

Snake
1. *That salesman has the reputation of a **snake**.*
2. My favorite **snake** at the zoo is a python.
3. This line to get into Disneyland will **snake** around for about two hours.
4. The plumber used a **snake** to unclog the drain.

Snarl
1. *That wild dog will **snarl** if you get too close.*
2. I am trying to comb this **snarl** out of your hair.

Snag
1. *Tracy rushed into the store to try to **snag** the last pair of shoes that were on sale.*
2. Our group hit a **snag** when our team leader was transferred to another department.

©2006, RULES

3. I have a **snag** in my new stockings.

Sneeze
1. *Charlotte will **sneeze** if she smells the flowers.*
2. Mike's **sneeze** was so loud, it startled me.
3. The money you made is nothing to **sneeze** at.

Initial /sm/ blends

CD 4:24

small ★	smile ★	smell ★
smog	smash ★	smoke ★
smooth ★	smother	smudge
smug	smart ★	smirk ★
smear ★	smelt	smithereens

Sentences and/or definitions:

1._____

2._____

Personal Words:

Small
1. *Is Iris **small** for her age?*
2. It is a **small**-scale operation.
3. We resolved the **small** problem yesterday.
4. She has pain in the **small** of her back.
5. I keep **small** change in my purse.

Smooth
1. *Elana's hair is **smooth** and silky.*
2. The character in my novel is very **smooth**.
3. What can I do to **smooth** the tension?

Smear
1. *If you touch this with your dirty hands, you will **smear** the glass.*
2. He wanted to **smear** her reputation by telling lies.
3. The biologist looked at the **smear** of cells on the slide.

Smash
1. *According to critics, the Broadway debut of the play was a **smash**.*
2. Be careful not to **smash** into each other on the trampoline.
3. He won the game with an overhead **smash**.

Smart

1. *The teachers said John was very **smart**.*
2. Yuki is an extremely **smart** dresser.
3. A wasp sting can **smart**.

Smell

1. *I **smell** something delicious in the kitchen.*
2. One's sense of **smell** can affect their sense of taste.

Smile

1. *Try to **smile** when you are giving a presentation.*
2. Kayla has a beautiful **smile**.

Smirk

1. *Why do you have that **smirk** on your face?*
2. When she gave the wrong answer, her brother looked at her with a **smirk**.

Smoke

1. *I see **smoke** coming out of the chimney.*
2. Doctors advise people not to **smoke**.
3. Let's **smoke** the salmon.
4. Why don't we go outside for a **smoke**?

Initial /sk/ blends

CD 4:25

scared	scan ★	skip ★
skill	schematic	skim ★
scale ★	sketch ★	scam
scatter	scallop ★	scarf ★
sky	scheme	skin ★

Sentences and/or definitions:

1. _____

2. _____

Personal Words:

Scale

1. *The doctor asked the pregnant woman to step on the **scale**.*
2. Will the chef **scale** the fish for me?
3. The athlete wanted to **scale** the mountain.
4. Is the architectural sketch drawn to **scale**?
5. Shannon warmed up her voice by singing in the **scale** of C.

Scan
1. *I have to have a CAT scan to see what is causing my pain.*
2. Can you please **scan** the crowd and see if you can find my dog?
3. Don't forget to **scan** the photo into the computer.

Sketch
1. *The comedian's sketch was amusing.*
2. Luca likes to **sketch** his designs before he paints them in oils.
3. Look at all of his drawings in his **sketch** book.

Scallop
1. *Would you like to try a grilled scallop?*
2. The pillow sham had a **scallop**-shaped edge.

Skip
1. *It is hard for children to learn how to skip.*
2. I think I'll **skip** the networking meeting tonight.
3. You can **skip** over the boring chapters.

Skim
1. *We have whole milk and skim milk in our refrigerator.*
2. I can't read all of my notes tonight; I'll just **skim** what I can.
3. Can you please **skim** the oil off the soup?

Scarf
1. *Hungry teenagers like to scarf their food.*
2. Kathleen knit a colorful **scarf** to match her coat.

Skin
1. *Exposed skin can get easily sunburned.*
2. The barbarian knew how to **skin** the animal.
3. I removed the **skin** before I grilled the chicken.

Initial /sw/ blends

CD 4:26

sweep ★	swim ★	sweat ★
swagger	swallow ★	sworn
swollen	swerving	swipe
swell ★	swelter	switch ★
Swiss ★	switchboard	swirl ★

Sentences and/or definitions:

1._____

Sweep
1. *The Red Sox beat the Yankees in a **sweep.***
2. Please **sweep** the kitchen floor when you are done eating.
3. With a dramatic **sweep** of her hands, the show was over.

Swell
1. *I **swell** with pride when I watch my daughters.*
2. Elevate your leg so it doesn't **swell**.
3. I told him it was a **swell** idea.

Swiss
1. *If you are from Switzerland, you are considered **Swiss**.*
2. Would you like Cheddar or **Swiss** cheese on your sandwich?

Swim
1. *Would you like to **swim** or bike this afternoon?*
2. I don't want to **swim** in perfume.
3. I love to take a **swim** in the ocean.

Swirl
1. *Would you like vanilla ice cream with a fudge **swirl**?*
2. Evie likes to **swirl** around on the dance floor.

Swallow
1. *Look through my binoculars to see the **swallow**.*
2. Please chew and **swallow** your food carefully.
3. I will **swallow** my pride and go.
4. I refuse to **swallow** that excuse!

Sweat
1. *Here is a towel to wipe off your **sweat**.*
2. Don't **sweat** if you can't finish by the deadline.
3. Your **sweat** glands work to keep you cool.
4. Jake broke out in a **sweat** when he was caught in a lie.

Switch
1. *I think we missed the exit; let's **switch** directions.*
2. Turn the light **switch** off.
3. Can I **switch** this medium sweater for a small?

Initial /skw/ blends

CD 4:27

square★	*squat*★	squall
squeak★	*squeeze*★	squint
squirt★	squander	squirm
squash★	squeamish	squid
squirrel★	squiggle	squeal ★

Sentences and/or definitions:

1._____

2._____

Personal Words:

Square
1. *The rooms in this old house are not perfectly **square**.*
2. My parents are not **square**; they are hip.
3. There is a lovely fountain in the town **square**.
4. Here is the money I owe you; now we are **square**.

Squirt
1. ***Squirt** the ketchup out of the squeeze bottle.*
2. I just need a **squirt** of ointment.
3. They called the little boy a "**squirt**."

Squash
1. *Do you play **squash** or racquetball?*
2. What type of **squash** do you like to eat?
3. If you put the juice on top of the raspberries, you will **squash** them!

Squirrel
1. *Look at that little **squirrel** in the tree.*
2. I am trying to **squirrel** away some money for taxes.

Squat
1. *My yoga teacher likes us to **squat** against the wall.*
2. The Sumo wrestler had a **squat** physique.
3. You cannot **squat** on land to claim it as your own.
4. The **squat** basement windows had a film of soot.

Squeeze
1. *You cannot **squeeze** that secret from me.*
2. Let's **squeeze** some oranges for breakfast.

3. He described his girlfriend as his "main **squeeze**."

Squeal
1. *I heard a **squeal** when I accidentally stepped on my cat's tail.*
2. It is not nice to **squeal** on someone.

Squeak
1. *A mouse will **squeak**.*
2. The old floor will **squeak** if you step on it.
3. I heard a **squeak** in the dark basement.

D. OTHER INITIAL BLENDS

Initial /tw/ blends

CD
4:28

tweed	twig	twinge
twelve	twenty	twice
twine	twilight ★	twin ★

Sentences and/or definitions:

1.＿＿＿＿＿＿＿＿＿＿＿＿＿＿＿＿＿＿＿＿＿＿＿＿＿＿＿＿

2.＿＿＿＿＿＿＿＿＿＿＿＿＿＿＿＿＿＿＿＿＿＿＿＿＿＿＿＿

Personal Words:

Twilight
1. *Elderly people are considered to be in the **twilight** of their lives.*
2. Have you ever looked at the ocean at **twilight**?

Twin
1. *Jacob was Talia's fraternal **twin**.*
2. My car has a powerful **twin** engine.

Initial /kw/ blends

CD
4:29

question ★	quiz ★	quench

queen★	quickly	quadrant
qualified	quotable	quirky

Sentences and/or definitions:

1._____

2._____

Personal Words:

Question
1. *Raise your hand if you would like to ask a **question**.*
2. Don't **question** her motives.
3. How did you vote on ballot **question** number six?

Queen
1. ***Queen** Elizabeth resides in London.*
2. I will try to capture your **queen** when we play chess.

Quiz
1. *We have a **quiz** every Monday.*
2. I will **quiz** you on the details when you return from your date.

E. FINAL CONSONANT CLUSTERS

Final /ld/ clusters

CD
5:1

cold★	held	told
yield★	failed★	cancelled
weld★	field★	sold
mild★	filled★	mailed
hold★	bold	gold★
installed	old	polled

Sentences and/or definitions:

1._____

2._____

Personal Words:

Cold

1. *It's unusually **cold** for the month of June.*
2. Why did Lorraine give you a **cold** stare when you walked into the room?
3. One of my roommates is **cold** and aloof.
4. Don't sit next to me because I woke up with a terrible **cold**.
5. Martin knew the rules and regulations **cold**.

Yield

1. *Our garden had a low **yield** of tomatoes this summer.*
2. Didn't you see the **yield** sign?
3. I will not **yield** to unreasonable demands.

Weld

1. *Sometimes they teach you how to **weld** metal together in shop class.*
2. They will **weld** their loving relationship by marriage.

Mild

1. *The weather is usually **mild** in the springtime.*
2. Katie has a **mild** temperament.

Hold

1. *Please **hold** onto the railing when you climb the steep steps.*
2. I can **hold** your keys.
3. Let's **hold** our meeting in my office.
4. Lindsay's domineering father has a **hold** on her emotions.
5. I've been on **hold** with customer service for over ten minutes!
6. I'm putting my travel plans on **hold** because of the airline strike.
7. The foul weather gear is stored in the ship's **hold**.
8. I'll **hold** the baby if she is fussy.

Field

1. *Look at the beautiful flowers growing in the **field**.*
2. Where is the high school football **field**?
3. Wendy works in the speech pathology **field**.
4. My dad taught me how to **field** a baseball.
5. Deb will **field** questions after her talk.

Failed

1. *Jim **failed** to see the point I was trying to make.*
2. Jordan **failed** chemistry and repeated it in summer school.
3. The fighter pilots turned around and had a **failed** mission.

Filled

1. *At the company picnic, the table was **filled** with tasty food.*
2. Yohanna **filled** the bathtub with fragrant oils.
3. The house was **filled** with the sound of laughter.
4. I'm sorry, but we have **filled** all of the available tables for the auction.
5. Yoko **filled** her prescription at the pharmacy.
6. Mr. Shield **filled** in for the absent instructor.

Gold

1. *Do you like **gold** or silver jewelry?*
2. What is the current value of an ounce of **gold**?
3. Rosie's hair was **gold**-colored.

Final /lt/ and /lts/ clusters

CD 5:2

belt ★	built ★	vault ★
fault ★	felt ★	quilt ★
melt ★	wilt ★	tilts
salt	adult	dealt ★
bolt ★	asphalt	cobalt
colts	faults	somersaults

Sentences and/or definitions:

1. _____

2. _____

Personal Words:

Quilt

1. *Lisa made a patch-work **quilt** for the new baby.*
2. The women would **quilt** every Wednesday afternoon.

Belt

1. *I am looking for a brown leather **belt**.*
2. How many years did it take for you to earn a black **belt**?
3. Parts of Ohio are considered to be in the Rust **Belt**.
4. Grace likes to **belt** it out when she sings.
5. The alcoholic liked a **belt** of scotch when he awoke everyday.

Fault

1. *It wasn't your **fault** that the glass broke.*
2. I would prefer not to live on a **fault** line.
3. I don't think being direct is a character **fault**.
4. Two serves into the net is a double **fault** in tennis.
5. I don't **fault** you for forgetting my birthday.

Melt

1. *I **melt** when I look into his beautiful eyes.*
2. If you leave chocolate in the hot sun, it will **melt**.
3. Your cares will **melt** away when you are on vacation.
4. I would love to have a tuna **melt** for lunch.

Bolt

1. *Did you see that **bolt** of lightning?*
2. Please **bolt** the fence so the animals can't escape.
3. The decorator showed us a **bolt** of beautiful fabric.
4. A nut goes with a **bolt**.
5. I had to **bolt** to my car before I got a ticket.

Built

1. *That athlete is well **built**.*
2. Our house was **built** in the 1920's.
3. The lawyer **built** a strong defense based on the evidence.

Felt

1. *I **felt** sorry for the boy with the broken leg.*
2. This scarf is made out of **felt**.
3. I **felt** the soft kitten.

Vault

1. *The athlete tried to **vault** over the post.*
2. Do you keep wine in your **vault**?
3. Matt competed in the pole **vault** event.

Wilt

1. *The flower will **wilt** if it doesn't have water.*
2. I will **wilt** in this heat.

Dealt

1. *Mark **dealt** with a lot of adversity in his life.*
2. The card dealer **dealt** out a great hand of cards.

Final /lf/ clusters

CD
5:3

shelf ★	itself	himself
herself	golf	wolf
gulf	self	elf
yourself	pelf	Rolf
half**	calf ** ★	

** "l" is silent in these words.

Sentences and/or definitions:

1._____

2._____

©2006, RULES

Personal Words:

Shelf

1. *The librarian put the book back on the **shelf**.*
2. What is the **shelf** life of this tuna?
3. The craft supplies were available off the **shelf**.

Calf

1. *I sprained my **calf** when I went running.*
2. The **calf** is suckling its mother.

Final /lm/ clusters

film★	*realm*	*balm***
*calm***★*	*palm***★*	*psalm****
overwhelm	*elm*	*helm ★*

** "l" is silent in these words.

Sentences and/or definitions:

1. _____

2. _____

Personal Words:

Film

1. *Please load the **film** into the camera.*
2. There is a **film** of dirt on this window.
3. The **film** was screened at the Cannes Film Festival.
4. The photographer will **film** the models in Greece.

Calm

1. *There was an eerie **calm** before the storm.*
2. I feel relaxed and **calm** after a steam and sauna.
3. Please **calm** down and listen to me.

Palm

1. *That coconut fell from a **palm** tree.*
2. A **palm** reader will study your hand carefully.

Helm
1. *Tony is at the **helm**, guiding the boat ashore.*
2. The CEO is definitely at the **helm** of this organization.

Final /lk/ clusters

CD
5:5

milk ★	*silk*	*bulk* ★
sulk	*hulk*	*talk*** ★
*walk*** ★	*stalk*** ★	*caulk***
*chalk***	*yolk***	*folk***

** *"l" is silent in these words*

Sentences and/or definitions:

1._____

2._____

Personal Words:

Milk
1. *Would you like **milk** or cream in your coffee?*
2. I will try to **milk** the situation to my advantage.
3. Do you know how to **milk** a cow?

Walk
1. *Please **walk**; don't run!*
2. We took a nice **walk** around the neighborhood.
3. If we can't negotiate a better deal, we'll have to **walk**.

Stalk
1. *I need to chop a **stalk** of celery for the soup.*
2. He said he likes to **stalk** famous women.

Bulk
1. *It is more cost effective to buy items in **bulk**.*
2. The weightlifter took special vitamins to **bulk** up.

Talk
1. *Elinore's **talk** was about human genetics.*
2. Joanne and Lynda try to **talk** on the phone daily.
3. Would you like to **talk** about your concerns?

CD
5:6

help ★	*kelp*	*yelp* ★
scalp ★	*pulp* ★	*gulp* ★

Sentences and/or definitions:

1._____

2._____

Personal Words:

Help
1. *Maybe we should hire extra **help** for the summer.*
2. May I **help** you?
3. Take some aspirin; it should **help** your headache.
4. He screamed, "**Help**!" when he slipped on the ice.

Scalp
1. *Some people try to **scalp** their tickets at the door.*
2. I need special shampoo because my **scalp** is itchy.

Pulp
1. *When you lose a baby tooth, you can see the **pulp**.*
2. I like to drink orange juice without the **pulp**.
3. You need wood **pulp** to manufacture paper.

Gulp
1. *Eric took a long **gulp** and then spoke to the crowd.*
2. You will get a stomach ache if you **gulp** your drinks.

Yelp
1. *The dog will **yelp** if he steps on a thorn.*
2. A **yelp** is a sound of distress.

Final /pt/ clusters

CD 5:7

adept	wept	crept
accept ★	except ★	leapt
adapt	snapped ★	wrapped ★
typed	wiped ★	hoped
stepped	shipped ★	flipped ★

Sentences and/or definitions:

1._____

2._____

Personal Words:

Accept
1. *I **accept** the terms of the re-negotiated contract.*
2. We gladly **accept** your invitation to the wedding.
3. Sarah must **accept** responsibility for the broken vase.

Except
1. *Everyone can go, **except** Maya.*
2. I would have paid for the movie, **except** I left my wallet at home.

Snapped
1. *The old teacher **snapped** at her students.*
2. The dog **snapped** at the playful boy.
3. My cracker **snapped** when I took a bite.
4. My coat **snapped** in the front.

Wiped
1. *The mechanic **wiped** the grease off of his hands.*
2. Lily **wiped** the dusty furniture with a rag.
3. I accidentally **wiped** out the files on my computer.
4. The mother gently **wiped** her daughter's tears.
5. Nikki **wiped** out on her snowboard.

Wrapped
1. *The movie **wrapped** last night and is now ready to be edited.*
2. Helen **wrapped** all of the gifts in handmade paper.
3. The burn victim was **wrapped** in gauze bandages.
4. He **wrapped** up the discussion so we could end the meeting.
5. Carissa **wrapped** her arms around Jeremy.

©2006, RULES

Flipped

1. *Doug patiently **flipped** the pancakes for everyone's breakfast.*
2. Janie **flipped** through the magazines, until it was time for her appointment.
3. The referees **flipped** a coin to see who would receive first.
4. Rachel **flipped** when she got a scholarship to Cambridge University.

Shipped

1. *The soldiers from this area **shipped** out this morning after a tearful goodbye.*
2. We **shipped** the care package to the campers.

Final /ft/ clusters

CD
5:8

raft	craft★	sift★
rift	left★	cleft★
laughed	loft★	coughed
lift★	aft	gift★
drift★	bereft	daft

Sentences and/or definitions:

1._____

2._____

Personal Words:

Lift

1. ***Lift** up the lid of the box to see the present.*
2. They took the **lift** to the fourth floor.
3. Seeing your smiling face gives me a **lift**.

Drift

1. *The boat will **drift** away if you don't tie it to the post.*
2. The strong wind caused a snow **drift**.
3. Don't **drift** off to sleep after dinner.
4. Listen to me. Do you get my **drift**?

Craft

1. *What is your **craft**?*
2. There were small **craft** warnings due to the impending storm.

Left

1. *There was no food **left** after the party.*
2. Turn **left** at the second driveway.
3. My **left** hand is clumsier than my right.

Loft

1. *Maggie and Natalie live in a **loft** in New York City.*
2. Milt drove the golf ball with a high **loft**.

Sift

1. *Don't forget to **sift** the flour before you add it to the recipe.*
2. John will **sift** through the trash to find the lost ring.

Cleft

1. *Michael had a notable **cleft** in his chin.*
2. Kaitlin was born with a **cleft** palate.

Gift

1. *What should we bring Annie for a housewarming **gift**?*
2. Her grandmother will **gift** her family the cottage when she dies.
3. Mariel, Nikki, and Mike have the **gift** of athleticism.

Final /st/ clusters

CD 5:9

baste★	fist	coast★
specialist	cyst	most
twist★	scientist	wrist
worst	first	last★
test	post★	list★

Sentences and/or definitions:

1._____

2._____

Personal Words:

Twist

1. ***Twist** the twine to make it hold tightly.*
2. Do you remember how to dance the **Twist**?
3. Be careful not to **twist** your back when you lift something heavy.
4. I'll take a **twist** of lime in my drink.

Post

1. *Tie the horse up to the **post**.*
2. I will **post** the letter in tomorrow's mail.

Coast

1. *Jim tried to **coast** along this semester and did very little work.*
2. Karen lives along the **coast** in Maine.

Last

1. *He wished the vacation could **last** forever.*
2. Lee was the **last** one to finish the experiment.

List

1. *Don't forget to add his name to the **list**.*
2. **List** all of the projects that must be completed.
3. Write that down on the shopping **list**.

Baste

1. *When you're cooking a turkey, you have to **baste** it frequently so it won't dry out.*
2. The seamstress will **baste** the dress together before she sews it carefully.

Final /sts/ clusters

costs	*lasts*	crusts
casts★	*roasts*★	hosts
guests	*trusts*	pastes
tastes	*wastes*	tests ★

Sentences and/or definitions:

1. _____

2. _____

Personal Words:

CD
5:10

Casts

1. *The fisherman **casts** out his fishing line from his boat.*
2. The **casts** of Broadway shows often have a special party on opening night.
3. The orthopedic (or orthopaedic) surgeon **casts** broken bones in his office.
4. After the car accident, Joe had two **casts**; one on his arm and one on his ankle.

Roasts

1. *The Friar's Club in New York City is well-known for its celebrity **roasts**.*
2. We are having so many guests for dinner; we better put two **roasts** in the oven.
3. Larry **roasts** chicken on Sunday evenings.

Tests

1. *I had to take many **tests** to get into that program.*
2. The technician ran several **tests** before they were convinced the machine was safe.
3. Running **tests** my cardiovascular fitness level.

Final /sks/ clusters

CD 5:11

discs	risks★	asks
tasks	basks	kiosks
asterisks	desks★	masks★
tusks	whisks★	frisks

Sentences and/or definitions:

1._____

2._____

Personal Words:

Desks
1. *Lois is in charge of the New York and Los Angeles travel **desks** for that magazine.*
2. We need to move the **desks** out of the classroom so they can polish the floors.

Whisks
1. *The cooking school has enough **whisks** for all of the students.*
2. Russell **whisks** the girls off to school every morning.
3. Joanne **whisks** the eggs in the mixing bowl.

Masks
1. *The children wore Halloween **masks** with their costumes.*
2. The women received mud **masks** at the spa.
3. Taking pain medication often **masks** the real problem.

Risks
1. *Do you like to take **risks**?*
2. She **risks** losing her job if the company relocates.

Final /sp/ and /sps/ clusters

CD 5:12

wasp	cusp	lisp
crisp★	wisps	grasps
clasps	gasps	asps

Sentences and/or definitions:		
1._____		
2._____		
Personal Words:		

Crisp

1. *We bake cherry **crisp** every summer.*
2. The autumn air is **crisp** and refreshing.
3. The crackers were so **crisp** that they broke when we spread the cheese.

Final /kt/ clusters

act★	fact	effect★
project★	abstract★	direct★
predict	inspect	subtract
affect★	correct★	conflict★
depict	restrict	strict

Sentences and/or definitions:

1._____

2._____

Personal Words:

CD
5:13

Act

1. *What happens in **Act** III?*
2. Please **act** responsibly when you drive.
3. Joan likes to **act** in dramatic plays.

Project

1. *The financial department has to **project** end of year earnings.*
2. Don't **project** your anger toward your mother on me.
3. *We worked on a new **project** for the second quarter.* (different intonation pattern)

Abstract

1. *The Museum of Modern Art has many **abstract** paintings and sculptures on display.*
2. The authors will submit an **abstract** for the conference program.

Correct
1. *Elaine asked her secretary to **correct** her typing mistakes.*
2. I hope this is the **correct** address for the doctor's office.
3. Charlotte answered, "**Correct**," in agreement.

Affect
1. *The cold weather will **affect** the crop of citrus fruits.*
2. *Jeffrey's **affect** was cold and distant.* (different intonation pattern)

Effect
1. *We'll bring the plan into **effect** on the first of the year.*
2. What is the **effect** of temperature on inflated balloons?

Conflict
1. *The board meeting might **conflict** with our dinner plans.*
2. *We tried to settle the **conflict** amicably.* (different intonation pattern)

Direct
1. *I like people who are **direct** and honest.*
2. Can you please **direct** me to the admissions office?

Final /mp/ and /mpt/ clusters

lamp	bump★	slump
lump★	stomp	damp★
camp★	stamp★	plump★
limp★	cramp★	pump★
stamped	bumped	stump★

Sentences and/or definitions:

1._____

2._____

Personal Words:

Lump
1. *Claire needed to have a benign **lump** removed.*
2. Let's **lump** all the laundry together in this pile.
3. Would you like one **lump** or two in your iced tea?

Camp
1. *What **camp** will your children be attending this summer?*
2. Do you like to **camp** in the woods?
3. We can **camp** here until the rain stops.

©2006, RULES

Limp

1. *Why does that old man walk with a **limp**?*
2. My hair is **limp** in humid weather.
3. We'll have to **limp** along with inadequate staffing until the budget is approved.

Bump

1. *The baby got a **bump** on her forehead when she fell.*
2. Be careful not to **bump** into the sliding glass door.
3. A speed **bump** was set up in the neighborhood to slow down traffic.

Stamp

1. *May I see that beautiful **stamp** in your collection?*
2. The inspectors must put a **stamp** on your passport.
3. James can **stamp** his feet very loudly.
4. How can we **stamp** out homelessness in our country?

Cramp

1. *Did you get a **cramp** when you were swimming?*
2. I don't want to **cramp** your style, but may I make a suggestion?

Slump

1. *Our college basketball team is in a **slump**.*
2. Our store has seen a **slump** in sales since the beginning of the summer.
3. People who **slump** have poor posture.

Plump

1. *Some babies are very **plump**.*
2. That actress will **plump** up her lips with a collagen injection.

Pump

1. *The sign says, "Please pay at the **pump**."*
2. Have you seen my other black **pump**?
3. This old well has a hand **pump**.
4. I need to **pump** some air into my bicycle tires.
5. Body builders go to the gym to **pump** iron.

Stump

1. *Careful, don't trip on that tree **stump**!*
2. Did your teacher try to **stump** you on the final exam?
3. The politician made his usual **stump** speech along the campaign trail.
4. The amputee had phantom pain in his **stump**.

Final /nt/ clusters

CD
5:15

NOTE: These words can also be produced as an unreleased /t/.

ant	plant	meant
account★	complaint	document★
distant	cement★	intent
important	bent	supplant
stunt	discount★	scant

Sentences and/or definitions:

1._____

2._____

Personal Words:

Account
1. *I have a checking and a savings **account**.*
2. The witness gave her **account** of the robbery to the jurors.
3. On **account** of the rain, the party had to be postponed.
4. The partner got to choose which **account** she wanted to keep.

Cement
1. *The construction worker poured **cement** into the building's foundation.*
2. Let's **cement** this agreement with a written contract.

Document
1. *I would like to study the **document**.*
2. *The teacher will **document** how many days the students are late.* (different intonation pattern)

Discount
1. *Can we get a **discount** if we buy a series of tickets?*
3. *I will **discount** what you just said.* (different intonation pattern)

Final /nd/ clusters

CD 5:16

and	mend ★	tend ★
kind ★	wind ★	send
fund ★	trend	remind
found ★	friend	band/banned ★

Sentences and/or definitions:

1._____

2._____

Personal Words:

Fund
1. *Jim made sure to **fund** his IRA before the end of the tax year.*
2. Maggie contributed money to the Firefighter's **Fund**.

Kind
1. *What **kind** of movies do you prefer?*
2. Mel was a **kind** and considerate person.

Wind/Wind
1. *I can **wind** the rope around the post to keep it secure.*
2. The child played with a **wind**-up toy.
3. Before batteries, we used to **wind** watches to make them keep correct time.
4. *The wind is blowing very hard.*

Found
1. *Anne **found** some money in the sand at the beach.*
2. Go to the "Lost and **Found**" to see if someone turned in your jacket.

Mend
1. *Barry had the flu, but he is on the **mend**.*
2. I will **mend** your jacket if you give me some needle and thread.

Tend
1. *Karin likes to **tend** to her garden.*
2. I **tend** to eat late most evenings.

Band
1. *Marjorie lost her wedding **band** at the beach.*
2. The **band** played for three hours.
3. Hold the package together with a rubber **band**.

Final /dz/ clusters

finds ★	decides	leads ★
feeds	loads ★	collides
ends ★	friends	depends
sends	rides ★	aids/AIDS/aides ★
suspends	crowds ★	spreads ★

Sentences and/or definitions:

1._____

2._____

Personal Words:

Loads
1. *Henry **loads** bales of hay onto the truck every morning.*
2. I have six **loads** of laundry to do this weekend.
3. Some kids get **loads** of homework every night.

Rides
1. *Which **rides** do you like at Disneyworld?*
2. Cathy **rides** a bicycle to work instead of taking the bus.
3. Sarah **rides** her horse everyday.
4. I heard that the high school science teacher **rides** his students pretty hard.

Crowds
1. *I hate it when everyone **crowds** the front of the train so new passengers can't get on.*
2. The **crowds** at the July 4th concert were incredible.

Leads
1. *Which player **leads** for most runs batted in?*
2. He **leads** a simple life in the country.
3. The conductor **leads** the orchestra.
4. That actress always gets the **leads** in the community theatre.
5. She **leads** the members of her team by example.
6. You must connect the **leads** if you want the instrument to operate.
7. The male partner **leads** the female in ballroom dancing.
8. The police officer followed the **leads** of the witness.

Finds
1. *Janie and Marjorie looked for antique **finds** at the flea market.*
2. Julia **finds** organizational behavior an interesting subject.

©2006, RULES

Ends

1. *Who said, "The **ends** justify the means?"*
2. The story **ends** without revealing the protagonist's secret.

Aids / Aides / AIDS

1. *Charlotte **aids** the elderly by volunteering at the Senior Center.*
2. Lee purchased two hearing **aids** and keeps them in her dresser drawer.
3. The teachers' **aides** are an instrumental part of the educational team.
4. A significant amount of money has been donated for **AIDS** research.

Spreads

1. *The hostess served many different kinds of **spreads** for the crackers.*
2. A cold virus **spreads** very quickly.
3. The artist **spreads** out her supplies before she begins to paint.

Final /ts/ clusters

CD
5:18

lots★	shots★	hats
sits★	waits	sheets★
boots★	shoots★	fights★
lights★	starts★	wets

Sentences and/or definitions:

1._____

2._____

Personal Words:

Lots

1. *The parking **lots** were plowed after the snowstorm.*
2. Jared collected **lots** of baseball cards.
3. They drew **lots** to see who would present first.

Sits

1. *The dog **sits** on the driveway and watches the cars pass by.*
2. His decision to collect donations **sits** well with me.
3. The old house **sits** high on the hill.
4. Sue **sits** for the children every Wednesday afternoon.

Boots

1. *Don't forget to wear **boots** when you go out in the snow.*
2. The policeman placed **boots** on the illegally parked vehicles.
3. Leng **boots** up the computer as soon as he arrives at work.

Lights

1. *Turn off the **lights** before you go upstairs.*
2. Joanne separated the laundry into **lights** and darks.
3. Larry **lights** the candles on the birthday cake.

Shots

1. *Mikel takes **shots** at the basket thirty minutes each day.*
2. The little girl received all of her **shots** before entering kindergarten.
3. Jessie's friends drank **shots** of vodka to celebrate her twenty-first birthday.
4. We heard **shots** in the dark when we went camping.

Shoots

1. Jack **shoots** baskets like a pro.
2. The panda bear eats bamboo **shoots** for meals.
3. The rocket **shoots** through the sky.
4. Derek **shoots** his gun at the shooting range.

Starts

1. *Joanne **starts** the fire on the grill at 5:00.*
2. The movie **starts** at eight o'clock.
3. I hope Nikki **starts** in the soccer game today.

Sheets

1. *Please change the **sheets** on the bed before the guests arrive.*
2. During the summer storm, **sheets** of rain came down on the sunbathers.
3. Lee turned the **sheets** of music as Mike played the piano.

Fights

1. *Larry watched the **fights** on HBO last evening.*
2. It aggravates Harriet when JB **fights** with his younger brother.

Final /ʃt/ or "sht" clusters

CD
5:19

polished★	wished	cashed
splashed★	squashed	washed
pushed★	crushed★	flushed★

Sentences and/or definitions:

1. _____

2. _____

Personal Words:

©2006, RULES

Polished
1. *Bernice **polished** all of the sterling silver in her dining room.*
2. Elena looked **polished** for her college interview.

Pushed
1. Sasha likes to be **pushed** on the swing in the park.
2. Debbie was **pushed** to succeed at an early age.

Flushed
1. *Ellen looked **flushed** and feverish this morning.*
2. The toilet made an awful sound when it was **flushed**.
3. The nurse **flushed** the wound with saline solution.

Splashed
1. *The children **splashed** in the pool.*
2. We **splashed** the fire with a bucket of water.

Crushed
1. *Do you need whole or **crushed** tomatoes for the recipe?*
2. Sam was **crushed** when his team lost the championship.
3. The jeweler **crushed** the rock to look for stones buried inside.
4. Lee's kneecap was **crushed** in the car accident.

Final /tʃt/ or "cht" clusters

---

bleached★	*switched*	clenched
fetched	*stretched*	attached
dispatched	*matched*★	ditched

Sentences and/or definitions:

1._____

2._____

Personal Words:

CD
5:20

Bleached
1. *Grace's hair was **bleached** from the summer sun.*
2. This shirt was **bleached**, but the spots didn't come out.

Matched
1. *The rival gymnasts were **matched** in height and weight.*
2. The pillow cases and the sheets **matched**.
3. The medical student was **matched** with a residency program in New York.

Final "mb" clusters

CD
5:21

In some cases, you do not pronounce both letters of a consonant cluster. For example, when "b" follows "m" at the end of the word, only the "m" is pronounced. Say the following words aloud, making sure that the "b" is silent and <u>NOT</u> pronounced as a consonant cluster.

crumb	*thumb★*	*dumb*
numb	*limb★*	*succumb*
comb ★	tomb	climb
lamb	womb	bomb ★
jamb	plumb	

Sentences and/or definitions:

1._____

2._____

Personal Words:

Comb

1. *The **comb** on the bird's head was red.*
2. I like to **comb** my hair when it is wet.
3. May I borrow your **comb**?

Thumb

1. *I'll **thumb** through the racks and see if I can find something suitable to wear.*
2. I sprained my **thumb** playing racquetball.

Limb

1. *Sara went out on a **limb** for Jamie.*
2. The tree **limb** broke during the hurricane.
3. His lower **limb** strength increased after weightlifting.

Bomb

1. *That new play was a **bomb** and it closed within two weeks.*
2. The building was evacuated due to a **bomb** threat.
3. They plan to **bomb** the territory at dusk.

©2006, RULES

CD 5:22

widths	myths	goldsmiths
silversmiths	locksmiths	breaths
baths	paths ★	cloths
moths	tablecloths	growths
booths ★	tollbooths	births
earth's	mouths ★	months

Sentences and/or definitions:

1._____

2._____

Personal Words:

Booths

1. *There were thirty **booths** at the flea market.*
2. The hostess asked if we wanted to sit at tables or **booths**.
3. The voting **booths** were in the firehouse for Election Day.

Paths

1. *The **paths** in the forest are overgrown with weeds.*
2. I hope to see you if our **paths** cross again in the future.

Mouths

1. *The single mother had seven hungry **mouths** to feed.*
2. Anyone who **mouths** off to a teacher will get detention.
3. The theatre director **mouths** lines to the actors on stage if they forget what they were supposed to say.

CD 5:23

think ★	blink ★	bank ★
blank ★	honk	rink

| skunk | pranks | monks |
| links ★ | mink | sinks ★ |

Sentences and/or definitions:

1._____

2._____

Personal Words:

Think

1. *I think the show starts at 8 p.m., but I'm not positive.*
2. How can I possibly **think** when there are so many distractions!
3. Jed worked at the **think** tank in Washington, D.C.

Blank

1. *I wanted to introduce my friend, but my mind went blank!*
2. Don't give him a **blank** check.
3. Here is a **blank** sheet of paper to write on.
4. Why does Lucy have a **blank** expression on her face?
5. He will shoot a **blank** for target practice.

Sinks

1. *Sarah has two sinks in her kitchen.*
2. A small boat **sinks** quickly.
3. Peter **sinks** a small fortune into the new property.

Shrink

1. *What does your shrink think about all of this turmoil in your family?*
2. Wash the sweaters in cold water so they don't **shrink**.

Bank

1. *Is the bank open on Saturday?*
2. This fertility center has a sperm **bank**.
3. Don't **bank** on hearing from the admissions office until after the New Year.
4. Let's eat by the river **bank**.

Trunk

1. *In the old days, people traveled with a steamer trunk instead of a suitcase.*
2. Is there a spare tire in the **trunk** of the car?
3. What can an elephant do with its **trunk**?
4. The **trunk** of a tree can tell its age.
5. Some exercises are designed to strengthen your **trunk**.

Final Clusters for Past Tense

CD
5:24

NOTE: As discussed in the unit on past tense endings, pronounce past tense verbs using a final consonant cluster.

begged (gd)	jogged (gd) ★	hugged (gd)
robbed (bd)	grabbed (bd)	sobbed (bd)
waved / waived (vd) ★	lived (vd)	braved (vd)
waged (dʒd)	forged (dʒd) ★	merged (dʒd) ★
fizzed (zd)	crazed (zd)	seized (zd) ★
sipped (pt)	hoped (pt)	typed (pt)
ticked (kt)	baked (kt)	soaked (kt)
laughed (ft)	coughed (ft)	staffed (ft)
washed (ʃt)	fished (ʃt)	dished (ʃt)
watched (tʃt)	fetched (tʃt)	poached (tʃt)

Sentences and/or definitions:

1._____

2._____

Personal Words:

Merged

> 1. *The two companies **merged** at the end of the year.*
> 2. Juan had the accident when he **merged** into the left lane.

Jogged

> 1. *Lyle **jogged** around Central Park on Sunday mornings.*
> 2. His photographs **jogged** my memory of the traumatic event.

Forged

> 1. *Dylan **forged** ahead and completed the race.*
> 2. Kate **forged** his signature on the check.

Seized

> 1. *Martin **seized** the opportunity to meet the Senator.*
> 2. The agents **seized** the illegal drugs at the airport.

Waved/waived
1. *The kite **waved** in the breeze.*
2. We **waved** goodbye to our friends at the train station.
3. He **waived** the registration fee.

F. Middle Clusters

Middle Clusters

extra (ks)	*success (ks)*	*exercise (ks)* ★
examine (gz)	*exaggerate (gz)*	*example (gz)*
suggest (gʤ)	*recognize (gn)*	*significant (gn)*
environment (nm) ★	*government (nm)*	*exquisite (kskw)*
stigma (gm)	*complexity (ks)*	*Baltimore (lt)*

Sentences and/or definitions:

1._____

2._____

Personal Words:

Exercise
1. *It's important to **exercise** daily.*
2. That was an excellent **exercise** for self-control.

Environment
1. *Recycling is good for our **environment**.*
2. John works in a very hostile **environment**.

Grammar Rules

22. Articles and Demonstrative Pronouns

This section explains **definite (the)**, **indefinite (a, an)**, and **demonstrative articles/pronouns (this, that, these, those)**. These small words are often omitted, misused, or mispronounced. We do not typically stress these words in connected speech.

Definite Articles

A **definite article** (**the**) identifies and singles out a noun. The noun has already been mentioned, or the listener is familiar with it from previous knowledge or experience.

Definite articles are used with:

1. **Singular nouns**

 > **The** hurricane (Katrina) destroyed **the** French Quarter.

2. **Plural nouns**

 > **The** children enjoyed **the** activities at the museum.

3. **Noncountable nouns** - These nouns <u>DON'T</u> have plural forms. They represent <u>substances or concrete objects</u> (air, gas, liquids, sugar, hair, meat), <u>abstract concepts</u> (happiness, health, truth), <u>sports and games</u> (soccer, tennis, swimming, checkers, poker, gin rummy) and <u>weather</u> (wind, snow, rain, hail).

 > **The** orange juice was fresh-squeezed this morning.

 > She was late due to **the** traffic on the turnpike.

4. Proper nouns

- Oceans (The Pacific Ocean)
- Rivers (The Colorado River)
- Buildings (The World Trade Center)
- Bridges, Tunnels (The Verrazano Bridge, The Lincoln Tunnel)
- Hotels (The Sheraton)
- Theaters (The Kennedy Center)
- Museums/Galleries (The Smithsonian, The Metropolitan Museum of Art)
- Titles (The Vice President)
- Families (The Burke Family, The Smiths)
- Plural or multiple name countries or mountains (The United States of America, The U. S. Virgin Islands, The Netherlands, The People's Republic of China, The United Arab Emirates, The Appalachian Mountains, The Rocky Mountains)
- Names of teams (The Baltimore Ravens, The Philadelphia Sixers)
- Names of schools beginning with "University" (The University of Arizona vs. Arizona State University)

NOTE: The following nouns <u>DON'T</u> use definite articles: continents, lakes, streets, cities, names of mountains (singular), parks, most countries, states, and individual's names. However, when you refer to general terms, use an article. For example, We traveled to **the** mountains and camped in **the** parks.

Ø John visited **the** Empire State Building in Ø New York City.

The Wilners saw **the** Atlantic Ocean, Ø Bear Mountain, and Ø Lake Champlain on their vacation to Ø New England. They traveled to **the** Rocky Mountains and Ø Yosemite Park in the fall.

5. Superlatives (the best, the most, the tallest)

Jake was **the** best salesman in the company.

Jeremy's presentation was **the** shortest one at the meeting.

6. Ordinals (the first, the second, the last)

Suzy was **the** first person to arrive at the meeting.

Joanne was **the** second runner to reach the finish line.

7. Specific part of a group (some of the players)

Twenty-one percent of **the** doctors were from India.

Some of **the** attendants at the conference left early.

8. Before modifiers that specify the following noun (the sole individual, the single answer, the main idea, the same results)

The chief complaint was about the room accommodations.

Karen had **the** best reason for coming to **the** national trade show.

9. Before words describing groups (for the poor, for the victims) **or some nationalities** (The Americans)

The fundraiser collected money for **the** victims.

The soup kitchen provided food for **the** needy.

The Irish enjoy celebrating St. Patrick's Day.

The Swiss are famous for their watches and chocolate.

10. With mechanical inventions or devices, when it is a general example, not a specific object, (the radio, the subway)

Shelly arrived at work late because she took **the** subway.

Rita listens to news on **the** radio while driving to work.

Sheng takes **the** taxi to work each day.

NOTE: "Television" does not always follow this rule.

11. Before locations with obvious activities (the beach, the hairdresser)

Please go to **the** store and pick up some milk.

Lisa went to **the** hairdresser on Saturday.

NOTE: We <u>DON'T</u> use definite articles in the following situations:

1. **Names of meals**

Yesterday, I ate in restaurants for Ø breakfast, Ø lunch, and Ø dinner.

2. **General ideas of places**, e.g., college, school, church, synagogue, temple, jail, vacation, work. When it is specific, we use the definite article.

Joanne went to Ø school during the week, Ø work in the evenings and Ø church on Sundays.

Sasha went to **the** school to pick up **the** work she missed.

3. **Names of schools**, e.g., Cornell University. When a school begins with "University," use the article "the," e.g., The University of Michigan.

©2006, RULES

Indefinite Articles

An **indefinite article** (**a**, **an**, **some**) classifies a noun and is used to represent a type, class, or group distinct from some other type, class or group. It is used with singular nouns (a, an) or plural nouns (some). "An" is used when it precedes a word beginning with a vowel. It is preferable, in most cases, to pronounce the article "a" as a schwa /ə/ or "uh." If it becomes too prominent in the sentence, it may be confusing to the listener.

Singular nouns - **A** hurricane can cause a lot of damage.

An elevator is needed in a tall office building.

NOTE: We <u>DON'T</u> use indefinite articles in the following situations:

1. **Plural nouns**

    Ø Vacations are a welcome break from our daily routines.

2. **Noncountable nouns** – These nouns <u>DON'T</u> have plural forms. They represent <u>substances or concrete objects</u> (air, gas, liquids, sugar, hair, meat), <u>abstract concepts</u> (happiness, health, truth), <u>sports and games</u> (soccer, tennis, swimming, (checkers, poker, gin rummy) and <u>weather</u> (wind, snow, rain, hail).

    Ø Gas is very expensive.

    I wish you Ø good health and Ø happiness in the coming year.

    I bought Ø milk and Ø eggs at the supermarket.

    Lee likes to make fresh Ø orange juice and home-made Ø ice cream.

3. **Proper nouns**

    Ø Hurricane Katrina was a devastating event.

    Ø Mt. Rushmore is a man-made attraction.

4. **Nouns in general terms** (either singular or plural)

> Ø Water is refreshing to drink after a long run. (in general)
>> vs.
>
> The scientists examined **the** water that came from the lead pipes.
> (specific water)

> The doctors studied Ø complications of cardiac surgery. (<u>all</u> of the complications)
>> vs.
>
> The doctors examined **the** most life-threatening complications of cardiac surgery in the elderly. (<u>specific</u> complications)

5. **Nouns of time,** (night, noon, midnight)

> Jim must be home by Ø midnight.

> I'll meet you at Ø noon.

6. **Names of seasons** when speaking in generalities

> I love to see the flowers bloom in Ø spring.

> Please make sure you have warm clothing for Ø winter.

7. **Names of meals**

> Let's meet for Ø breakfast tomorrow.

> Philip ate Ø dinner at 7:00.

8. **Types of transportation when preceded by the word "by"**

> They went to Boston by Ø plane.

9. **Types of communication when preceded by the word "by"**

> "Mark confirmed the meeting by Ø e-mail."

> "We'll talk by Ø telephone."

©2006, RULES

Demonstrative Determiners/Pronouns

In order to make a clear reference, we might use a demonstrative determiner/pronoun such as **this, that, these,** or **those**. They can be used in place of an article.

"**This**" and "**that**" are used with singular nouns, while "**these**" and "**those**" are for plural nouns. We use "**this**" and "**these**" to refer to objects that are closer to the speaker or closer in time. "**That**" and "**those**" are used with more distant objects or further in the past.

this book	these books	that book	those books
this car	these cars	that car	those cars

This memo (it's right here) is referring to the upcoming meeting.

That memo (I saw it yesterday or it's over there) was circulated around the office.

This child (the one near me) is well-behaved.

That child (over there) is not paying attention.

These meetings (like the one we are now attending) are always scheduled in the afternoon.

Those memos (over there or the ones we already read) were not very clear.

Pronunciation Rules for "This," "That," "These," and "Those"

CD
5:26

*Remember to pronounce the final sound in "**these**" and "**those**" as a "**z**" sound.*

*Make sure the vowel is different for "**this**" /ɪ/ and "**these**" /i/.*

*Remember to pronounce the "**th**" or /ð/ sound correctly!*

Pronunciation Rules for "A" and "An"

*Use **"an"** before items that start with vowels or begin with a silent /h/, such as **"an** occupation" or **"an** honor."*

*Use **"a"** before words beginning with consonants, such as **"a** class" or **"a** book."*

*When using the article **"an,"** remember to link the final "n" with the following vowel sound.*

an␣apple   **an␣invitation**   **an␣officer**

NOTE: *When a word begin with the vowel "u," but is pronounced with a "Y-insertion," we treat it as a consonant and use "a."*

a *university*   **a** *uniform*   **a** *unicorn*

*When using the article **"a,"** we do not typically stress the article and we pronounce it as "uh" [ə].*

a *book*   **a** *table*   **a** *message*

Pronunciation Rules When Linking Acronyms/Initializations

When using an indefinite article with an acronym/initialization that begins with a consonant, remember to pronounce it as an unstressed schwa /ə/.

*Carissa received **a** B.A. from Sarah Lawrence College.*

*Marty tries to contribute to **a** SEP (acronym) to prepare for retirement.*

When an acronym/initialization begins with a vowel or F, H, L, M, N, R, S, or X, use "an." These letters are actually pronounced with a vowel in the beginning, e.g. "EF," "AYCH," "EL," "EM," "EN," "ARE," "ES," and "EKS."

*We were hoping to obtain **an␣**NIH grant.*

*Sasha needs to see **an␣**ENT for her ear infection.*

*Kang received **an␣**MBA from Harvard University.*

Pronunciation Rules for "The"

When *"the"* precedes a word beginning with a vowel, it is pronounced like "thee," [ði] and it links with the following vowel-initiated word.

the⁀invitation   *the⁀oven*   *the⁀apple*

When *"the"* precedes a word beginning with a consonant, it is not usually stressed and it is pronounced like "thuh," [ðə].

the book   *the* meeting   *the* time

NOTE: When words begin with the vowel "u," but are pronounced with a "Y-insertion," we can say it <u>either</u> with "thee" or "thuh."

The [ði]⁀University of Maryland   *The [ðə] University of Maryland*

23. Prepositions

CD
5:27

> ***Prepositions*** *are words that are used with nouns, pronouns, or other words to form phrases that function as modifiers of verbs, nouns, or adjectives. They may be used to show* <u>location</u> *or* <u>place</u> *(at, to, in, from, on, under, over, out, through, toward, away, on top of, beneath),* <u>time</u>, *(before, after, on, at, in, during, while), and* <u>accompaniment</u> *(with, without). The scope of prepositions is extensive. Please refer to a grammar book for more detailed information.*
>
> *Typically, prepositions are* <u>not</u> *stressed within the sentence. Stress will be used in a contrastive situation, when the speaker is emphasizing the preposition to clarify a point; for example, "The papers are not in the pile; they are **next to** the pile."*

Exercise 1: The following are some common prepositions. Try to use them in sentences. Then, say a sentence contrasting the preposition. For example,
"The plane is flying above the **clouds**." (typical stress pattern)
"No, the plane is flying **below** the clouds."

above	across	after	against
around	at	before	behind
below	beneath	besides	between
by	down	during	for
from	in	near	on
out	over	to	toward
under	up	with	without

Exercise 2: Read the following pairs of sentences and stress the preposition in the second sentence to indicate contrastive stress. **NOTE**: The prepositions are underlined, but should not be stressed in the first example. Typically, the last important word in the sentence should be stressed. These stressed words are in bold.

1.   *Are you <u>in favor of</u> eliminating the tolls on the **turnpike**?*
       *No, I'm **against** it.*

2. *Did you bring up your questions <u>during</u> the **meeting**?*
*No, I brought them up **after** the meeting.*

3. *Would you like your coffee <u>with</u> cream and **sugar**?*
*No, I would prefer to drink it **without**.*

4. *Are we driving <u>towards</u> New York **City**?*
*No, we're driving **away** from it.*

5. *Is Sally walking <u>down</u> the **hill**?*
*No, I saw her walking **up** the hill.*

6. *Would you like to cut your hair <u>above</u> your **shoulders**?*
*No, I would like to keep it **below** my shoulders.*

7. *Is there a blanket <u>on</u> the **seat**?*
*No, but there is one **underneath** the seat.*

8. *Is Lynda walking <u>in front of</u> **Marj**?*
*No, she's walking **next to** her.*

9. *Is my cell phone <u>on top of</u> the **fax** machine?*
*No, it's **next to** the fax machine.*

10. *Can you give me a ride home <u>from</u> work **tomorrow**?*
*No, I'm sorry, but I can give you a ride **to** work.*

Putting It All Together

Putting It All Together

Summary Sheet
The following activities incorporate your understanding and use of a combination of rules for areas such as compound nouns, proper nouns, abbreviations, acronyms, and numbers. Follow the directions for the exercises and remember to use the proper stress patterns as indicated. **NOTE:** You have the authors' permission to copy this summary sheet <u>only</u> as a reference tool to remind you of the **RULES**.

Unit	Rule	Example
Compound Nouns	Stress the first word	**green**house **get**-away
Adjectives + Nouns	Stress the noun	green **house**
Phrasal Verbs	Stress the second word	Get **away** Get it **away**
Proper Nouns	In two-word proper nouns, stress the second word. Capitalize the first letter of each word	New **York** Eiffel **Tower** George **Washington** Rocky **Mountains**
Acronyms (sometimes used interchangeably with abbreviations)	Say it as a word	**PIN**
Initializations	Stress the last letter	SU**V** US**A**
Heteronyms Two-syllable words	Noun -stress first syllable Verb -stress last syllable	**pro**ject pro**ject**

Unit	Rule	Example
Heteronyms Three syllable words	Adjective or noun – stress First syllable and shorten the last syllable Verb – stress first syllable	**du**plicate ‾ • • **du**pli<u>cate</u> ‾ • —
-Y Insertion	For the letter "u" or the letters "ew", a /j/ or "Y" sound is often heard in the pronunciation.	Exec<u>u</u>tive Man<u>u</u>facture
Past Tense Endings	Final voiceless sounds (k, p, f, sh or /ʃ/, ch or /ʧ/, th or /θ/, s), add a "t" sound. Final voiced sounds (g, b, v, j or /ʤ/, th or /ð/, z), and final vowels, add a "d" sound. Final "t" and "d" consonants, add an extra [əd] sound.	walk<u>ed</u> (t)　　stopp<u>ed</u> (t) wash<u>ed</u> (t)　　cough<u>ed</u> (t) listen<u>ed</u>　　show<u>ed</u> lov<u>ed</u>　　begg<u>ed</u> want<u>ed</u> (əd)　need<u>ed</u> (əd) content<u>ed</u> (əd)
-S Endings	Final voiceless consonants, add /s/ sound. Final voiced consonants or vowels, add a /z/ sound. Words ending in s, z, sh or /ʃ/, ch or /ʧ/, zh or /ʒ/, j or /ʤ/, add [əz].	step<u>s</u>　　sit<u>s</u> make<u>s</u>　　lift<u>s</u> lab<u>s</u>　　goe<u>s</u> agree<u>s</u>　　leave<u>s</u> pric<u>es</u>　　priz<u>es</u> wish<u>es</u>　　church<u>es</u>

Unit	Rule	Example
Voicing and Syllable Length	A vowel is held longer before a voiced consonant than a voiceless consonant.	s<u>a</u>d (voiced) d<u>u</u>g sat (voiceless) duck
Rules for Numbers	Stress first part of "ten" numbers Stress the second part of "teen" numbers Exception: When counting, stress first part of "teen" numbers	**fif**ty dollars fif**teen** dollars **thir**teen, **four**teen, **fif**teen, **six**teen ....